BUILDING YOUR
EARLY YEARS BUSINESS

of related interest

How to Be a Great Leader in Early Years
Jennie Johnson
ISBN 978 1 84905 674 8
eISBN 978 1 78450 180 8

Leadership for Quality in Early Years and Playwork
Supporting Your Team to Achieve Better Outcomes for Children and Families
Debbie Garvey and Andrea Lancaster
ISBN 978 1 90581 850 1
eISBN 978 1 90581 883 9

A-Z of Being the Best Leader You Can Be
Leading Through the Alphabet
Yvonne Bleam
ISBN 978 1 78592 708 9
eISBN 978 1 78450 272 0

Performance Management in Early Years Settings
A Practical Guide for Leaders and Managers
Debbie Garvey
ISBN 978 1 78592 222 0
eISBN 978 1 78450 507 3

BUILDING YOUR EARLY YEARS BUSINESS

PLANNING AND STRATEGIES FOR GROWTH AND SUCCESS

Jacqui Burke

Jessica Kingsley *Publishers*
London and Philadelphia

First published in 2017
by Jessica Kingsley Publishers
73 Collier Street
London N1 9BE, UK
and
400 Market Street, Suite 400
Philadelphia, PA 19106, USA

www.jkp.com

Library of Congress Cataloging in Publication Data
A CIP catalog record for this book is available from the Library of Congress

British Library Cataloguing in Publication Data
A CIP catalogue record for this book is available from the British Library

ISBN 978 1 78592 059 2
eISBN 978 1 78450 319 2

Printed and bound in the United States

This book is dedicated to the two men whose belief in me will always be my source of courage and inspiration – my Dad and Mark.

ACKNOWLEDGEMENTS

My thanks go first of all to the team at Jessica Kingsley Publishers; writing a book wasn't something that I had considered doing and it was their encouragement that gave me the confidence to write this book. I would also like to thank Jeremy Webster of Silver Pebble; we have worked in partnership over the past five years in delivering training and qualifications to support early years business advisers, building a strong reputation throughout the country for this work. Thanks also to Sue O'Brien for helping with the illustrations, and to Ross Midgley and Charlotte Pace for technical advice.In particular I would like to thank all the early years business owners, managers and trustees who have shared their stories with me during the training sessions that they have taken part in over the past 12 years; your stories have added the colour to this book.

CONTENTS

There are supplementary materials which
can be downloaded at www.jkp.com/voucher
using the code BURKEBUSINESS

PREFACE

Sustainable early years businesses rely on highly committed people who share a passion for delivering a high quality childcare service. But having a passion for childcare isn't enough on its own. They also need to be managed by people who have a high level of business management capability. And in today's challenging financial climate, this is more than ever the case.

In the past early years business support teams from local authorities provided support to improve the business management skills of providers, but many issues remain. According to research conducted by the Office for Public Management (OPM) on behalf of 4Children and the DfE (Jackson and Fitzpatrick 2013) only 59 per cent of providers feel confident in their business skills. So does that mean that almost 40 per cent of the sector is being managed by people who aren't quite sure about how to run a business successfully?

Statistics also tells us that small businesses in general in the UK suffer from a lack of business management skills, and that this results in high levels of business failures, in the region of 40,000 each year. With close to half a million people employed in the early years sector, this places a burden of responsibility on those who manage early years businesses.

The early years sector probably suffers from a lack of business management capability more than many other sectors. I think this is because of the type of people who often find themselves running childcare settings, and their routes into business management roles; many started working in early years because it fitted in with their personal circumstances and because they love working with young children, and somehow over the years find themselves running a business, with all of the challenges and responsibility that entails.

Having drifted into the role, very few have received the sort of formalised business management training that people might access when they make a conscious decision to start up a business. Many just kind of muddle along on a day to day basis and hope they are getting things right – which is fine when things are running smoothly but not so great when the business faces problems. Others are acutely aware that they are out of their depth and don't know where to go for support, especially now that business support teams have been disbanded by many local authorities. Some don't even think of themselves as running a business. They put their heads in the sand and hope that someone else will take care of all this nasty business stuff so they can concentrate on looking after the children.

It is also the case that some are doing a great job and have massive potential, but lack the confidence to take their business to another level.

Early years business owners and managers need to recognise that improvements in the quality of their provision will come from being better able to manage their business.

Research that supports this message includes the London Councils' 2007 report that demonstrated that:

> Good business skills can improve the sustainability of childcare businesses which, in turn, can impact on affordability for parents and quality of provision. (p.8)

So this book is about helping settings to have the confidence to shift their self-perception away from the 'it's just childcare' label that so many currently wear and to focus on building their business management capability as a means to delivering high quality, sustainable childcare. It is intended to provide support to people in a range of roles including, but not limited to:

- early years business owners and senior managers

- committee members of voluntary sector pre-schools

- governors, head teachers and school business managers of schools intending to enter the early years market as an extension of their services

- registered childminders

- local authority employed business support advisers (and other local authority staff where business support is an element of their role)

- freelance business consultants who have clients in the early years sector.

Chapter 1

THE PRINCIPAL ELEMENTS OF A SUSTAINABLE EARLY YEARS BUSINESS

Many people running businesses compare their experience with being on a journey. So I'm going to use that analogy to introduce this first chapter, and because I conduct many of my journeys by car I'm going to encourage you to think about taking a car journey to assist our thinking.

Increasingly, modern technology has made it possible for the car driver to check out how their vehicle is performing without ever having to lift up the bonnet and get their hands dirty. The on-board computer in most modern cars provides the driver with a dashboard of key information delivered directly to them while comfortably in the driving seat. This means that the driver has at a glance all the information they need to tell them how their car is performing. Dials and logs provide information about fuel levels, speed, revs, temperature, average miles per litre etc. and various warning lights are illuminated to tell us when there is a problem that we need to address, usually lighting up amber initially so that we can sort the problem out before it causes any damage to the car. We have become so reliant on these on-board computers to tell us that everything is ok that most of us very rarely actually look under the bonnet and check things out for ourselves.

So think now about your early years business. How valuable would it be to have a dashboard that gives you the basic information about how your business is performing and which alerts you to things that you might need to pay attention to?

A balanced business scorecard approach to business planning and management is the answer to this wish.

The balanced scorecard approach was originally devised by Robert S. Kaplan and David Norton and was described by them in an article for the Harvard Business Review as a tool that retains traditional financial measures but acknowledges that financial measures alone don't tell the whole story as a tool to guide the journey that 21st century businesses undertake. Understanding the business in terms of customers, suppliers, employees, processes, technology, and innovation is equally important. In a nutshell (and to contradict pop singer Jessie J) it's not 'all about the money'. Through their research they found that many businesses have a tendency to focus their attention purely on the financial aspects of their performance. This is the equivalent in my car analogy of only ever looking at the fuel gauge to see if you've got enough left in the tank. This is too one dimensional. It's not the only measure that matters.

In early years settings it's often the case that business owners and managers may have come from a background of delivering childcare, rather than running a business, and so may inevitably feel more comfortable with managing those areas of the business, i.e. the quality of childcare provision. Again this single emphasis and focus is too one dimensional. They may fail to address fully some of the business-related issues which they typically find more challenging.

A balanced scorecard approach, or what I'm going to refer to as a dashboard approach, gives a more holistic view of the performance of your early years business by encouraging you to consider a range of key factors affecting the success of the business.

The dashboard approach to planning and management suggests that businesses shouldn't measure their success purely in financial terms, but that we should look at all of the factors that contribute to the success of the business. So, for example, you may have a great financial plan but if your relationship with your customers is poor you are unlikely to see great success.

The first step towards a dashboard is for the business to identify 4–6 areas in which it needs to be successful, what I call your key result areas, and to agree key goals for those areas. The dashboard framework I recommend is a slight variation on the original Kaplan and Norton model and includes the following elements:

- finance

- parents

- staff

- quality provision

- business effectiveness

- continuous improvement.

This framework is the basic premise that underpins this book. The various chapters in the book will help you to develop strategies for each of these elements to support the success and growth of your early years business.

The dashboard approach then encourages you to answer some critical questions about the performance of your business in each of these key result areas:

- What do you need to achieve in each of these areas to be successful (your goals)?

- How will you measure your performance in achieving each of these goals (key performance indicators or KPIs)?

- How are you doing so far (progress/current performance)?

- What do you need to focus on to keep on track (your action plan)?

A template to help you to create your early years business dashboard would typically look like the following table:

Key result area	Goals	KPIs	Progress/ current performance	Action plan
Finance	To break even by 30th July	Income to exceed £xxx Expenditure to be below £xxx	Monthly progress report	Marketing to fill vacancies Review staffing ratios/costs
Parents				
Staff				
Quality provision				
Business effectiveness				
Continuous improvement				

Tips for constructing your Early Years Business Dashboard

- Keep your focus strategic – this means focusing on the big picture things not the nitty gritty day to day details.

- Don't set too many goals – prioritise 3–4 for each key result area – otherwise you'll end up diluting your effort.

- Make sure your goals are aspirational and inspirational – they should feel like a stretch but not like an unachievable challenge, they should inspire you to come to work and achieve them.

- Select key performance indicators that can be measured objectively – you should be able to answer the question 'How will we know we've achieved our goal?'.

- For longer term goals set milestones along the way so you can check that you are on track – for example, a goal to be achieved in three years time needs a milestone of where you expect to be by the end of year 1 and year 2.

- Monitor your progress towards your goals regularly – some might be monthly, some quarterly and some annually.

- Ask your staff for their ideas about your action plan to build their commitment and engagement.

Using your dashboard to performance manage your early years business

Having created your dashboard it is essential that it is used on a day to day basis to manage the performance of your business, just as in my car analogy. The following section provides a suggested methodology for the practical implementation of an early years business dashboard, including how to use it as a part of your Self Evaluation Form (SEF).

The dashboard provides a clear focus on what's really important. And if cascaded to people throughout the business, it also provides everyone with clarity about where they fit into the picture, and how they contribute, which helps to build motivation and commitment through a shared sense of pride in the achievements of the business.

Making a dashboard approach come to life involves putting a number of key enablers into place:

- Getting a wide cross-section of your team involved in agreeing the performance measures ensures buy-in and builds understanding of each other's areas of responsibility.

- Make it real by cascading business objectives down into the work objectives of every individual within the business, making it a fundamental part of how people's performance is managed; this ensures that everyone is pulling in the same direction.

- Good IT systems allow the business to record and report on the critical data required with ease and accuracy.

I will make use of the dashboard structure that I've explained in this chapter to underpin the rest of the book. So do take a bit of time to create your own dashboard so that you can join me on that journey. The tools and techniques outlined in the next chapter will help you to do this.

Chapter 2

TOOLS AND TECHNIQUES FOR UNDERSTANDING YOUR EARLY YEARS BUSINESS

In this chapter I am going to explore a number of well-established tools and techniques that you can use to help you to analyse and understand more about your early years business, and to plan for future success and growth.

There are many tools and techniques that can help you to analyse the performance of your business and this section covers a few that I use a lot with my early years clients and find really useful. These tools are generic and can be used in any business in any sector but I'm going to explore how to use them in an early years context.

There is a temptation to rename tools and techniques to make them sound more 'early years friendly' but I really don't subscribe to this approach. I feel that a 'dumbing-down' of business language is condescending to early years providers and does nothing to build people's confidence in using such terminology. I will make sure that the use of each model, tool or technique is described using examples that you will be familiar with (rather than renamed). If I use any business language which I find my early years clients tend not to be familiar with, I will make a point of describing or explaining it in language that we tend to use in the sector.

SWOT Analysis

I'm going to begin with the SWOT Analysis, as this is a tool that most people leading early years businesses are familiar with.

It simply summarises your setting's strengths and weaknesses, plus the opportunities and threats you are faced with.

Although many people are familiar with this technique, the tendency is often to complete one as a bit of a 'back of an envelope' activity without any real analysis behind it. As a result, what is produced tends to be very superficial and therefore not very useful.

My approach is to use a SWOT Analysis as a summary of the results of a number of other pieces of analysis in order to create something more robust and meaningful, and therefore more valuable.

Strengths	Weaknesses
Good team, loyalty, long-service	Recent breakdown in communication between teams
Well established partnership with local childminders for out of hours care	New management structure not embedded yet
Relationship with primary school supports smooth transitions for children	Lack of clear roles and responsibilities
Sense of community within the village	Conflict of interest in senior management team
Good relationships with parents who take an active interest in the setting	Weak financial/business knowledge and skills
Ofsted Outstanding twice	

Opportunities	Threats
Further develop website/blog and social media presence	Loss of staff due to current internal tensions
Delegate responsibilities to grow skills	Low morale
Hold parents' evenings to improve communications	Reduction in LA support impacts on quality
New housing development approved	Higher costs result in financial difficulties

Tools that can be used to contribute towards your SWOT

As the chapters that follow make reference back to the tools discussed in this chapter I would encourage you to take some time having a go at completing each of these analyses for your own setting.

PESTLE Analysis – what's going on in the world around us

A PESTLE Analysis provides a framework to help you to identify what's going on in the world around you using six headings to prompt your thinking: political, economic, social, technological, legal and environmental.

I have lots of conversations with early years business owners about new legislation and other significant changes in their world which have caught them on the hop. A prime example of this in recent years has been the impending introduction of Auto-Enrolment Pension Arrangements. As I am writing this book in 2016, with the staging date for small businesses looming ever closer, I am still hearing setting owners ask, 'How can we be expected to manage this with such little notice – why weren't we told about this sooner?'

I often remind people that in actual fact the government began the process of introducing the scheme way back in the Occupational and Personal Pension Schemes (Automatic Enrolment) Regulations 2010. And this was predated by a consultation period going back to 2007 that resulted in the Pensions Act 2008. The problem is that for many early years business owners, this discussion and the resulting legislative changes went unobserved. The warnings were there all along, allowing plenty of time to prepare for the changes, but without settings being aware of the warning signs it feels like a sudden WHAM! The changes seem to be upon us with precious little time to plan and prepare for implementation.

Another example that I came across was of an early years business which was located in lovely semi-rural premises just outside a village in the Midlands. Ninety per cent of their customers came from the nearby village. So imagine their shock when they suddenly received notice that the planned route for the new HS2 railway would run in between their setting and the village where their customers live, creating a diversion of several miles for customers to be able to access them. Again, this came a complete shock to the setting owners, who hadn't taken the time to attend any of the consultation meetings (held over several years). In this case it's going to be a while before the line is built and the change happens, but they could have had longer to make the changes needed to their business, such as relocation, if they had been more aware of what was being proposed.

And the same can be said for so many other external factors that can heavily impact on a small business unless we anticipate and plan for the changes.

A PESTLE Analysis is a tool that can be used to help you to do just that – to anticipate and understand the external factors that might impact on your business so that you are in a position to plan how best to cope with those factors. How to avoid problems arising and how to minimise negative impacts on your business if there are factors that are outside of your control entirely.

And coping with those changes isn't all negative. It is true that completing a PESTLE Analysis can sometimes be a bit of a depressing experience as it identifies lots of external factors that pose a threat to the business which are totally outside of your control. But the planning you can do in this situation enables you to take back control, making your business as resilient as possible to things that might threaten it.

I would also stress that some of the external factors that you identify using your PESTLE Analysis will actually present opportunities for the future which might otherwise have been overlooked. Identifying these factors enables you to plan the best way to take advantage of those opportunities and turn them to the advantage of the business.

An example of this was shared with me recently by an early years business adviser who had helped a setting to choose a new location for her business. By helping her to understand the direction of travel of government policy, something she had never really taken much notice of before, she selected a location in an area that she would never previously have considered suitable for her setting. The business is now located in an area of high deprivation which is being targeted by the government, and is thriving as a result of being perfectly placed to offer provision to the troubled families in that area.

A PESTLE Analysis is especially useful at times when a business is planning to make changes such as starting-up, expanding or developing new services.

At the time of writing this book, early years and childcare continues to be very high on the political agenda, with announcements about significant future changes being made by government almost on a monthly basis. Early years business owners and managers need to have a mechanism for reviewing these regularly so that they can anticipate and plan for the impact that these changes might have on their setting. The PESTLE Analysis provides this tool.

I am often asked how frequently you should complete a PESTLE Analysis and the answer is – it depends. Certainly once a year it's worth reviewing and updating it as a part of your normal strategic business planning cycle. But if the world is in upheaval with lots of uncertainty (e.g. after the BREXIT vote), if the nature and pace of change in your early years business is significant, then you will need to complete one more frequently.

How to use a PESTLE Analysis

Using each of the headings, brainstorm what is happening in the world around you and try to anticipate what things will look like in 12 months' time. Think as broadly as you can – what's happening in the world in general, not just in the early years and childcare sector. Be specific about how those things might affect your early years business. Here are some questions to prompt your thinking:

POLITICAL

- Consider what is likely to happen in terms of national politics over the next 12 months – elections/referendums, regionalisation/devolution, current government policy relating to childcare/education/working parents, etc.

- Consider what is likely to happen in terms of local politics in your area over the next 12 months – local elections, possible changes to local government control, removal/merger of local authority services, local policy on childcare/education, etc.

- Consider what is likely to happen in terms of international politics over the next 12 months – EU expansion, BREXIT, refugees/migration, upheaval in Middle East and Africa, terrorist atrocities, etc.

ECONOMIC

- Consider what is likely to happen in the national economy over the next 12 months – are things improving, think about inflation/interest rates/national debt/GDP, etc.

- Consider what is likely to happen in terms of your local economy over the next 12 months – is your area thriving or in decline, is there inward investment creating new jobs or are jobs disappearing, is there a house building boom, is your area viewed as a desirable place to live, is it affluent or deprived, consider employment levels, etc.

- Consider what is likely to happen in terms of international economics over the next 12 months – exchange rates, the Euro, overseas trade, oil prices, etc.

- Consider the funding and other financial changes such as changes to apprenticeships affecting the sector.

SOCIAL

- Consider current trends in society such as working patterns, later retirement age, more self-employment, zero hours contracts and flexible working, single parent families, young people living with parents for longer, etc.

- Consider how society's attitudes towards early years provision are changing in terms of childcare vs. early education.

TECHNOLOGICAL

- Consider advances in technology and how they impact on the expectations of your various stakeholders, children, parents, local authority, central government departments, training providers, etc.

- Consider some of the issues impacting on your settings in terms of staff training, the cost of computer hardware and software, cyber threats and data security, internet connectivity, your online footprint (including social media).

LEGAL

- Consider some of the legislative changes that are likely to impact on your setting over the next 12 months – auto-enrolment, visa restrictions and other employment law changes post-BREXIT, etc.

- Also some of the early years specific changes that are coming in – 30 hours free entitlement, contracting to buy in traded services, etc.

Environmental

- Consider how changes in the environment might impact on your setting over the next 12 months – climate change, more extreme weather conditions, coastal and river erosion, fuel prices and shortages, government policy on recycling.

- Consider plans for major infrastructure changes that might impact on your settings depending on where you are located – HS2, Crossrail, new town development, the development of Enterprise Zones around the country.

Political	Economic	Social
BREXIT – unknown impact or timescales	Low interest rates and low inflation	Low unemployment so more women working – greater need for childcare and more job applicants
Local election – possible power shift	Fall in £ resulting in higher costs	
Austerity policy continues – removal of LA funding and support	NMW increases and pension contributions resulting in higher staff costs	Immigration resulting in a need for cultural and language awareness
Drive for schools to provide childcare	Rent and business rates increasing	New housing developments leading to increased demand
	New tax free childcare scheme	Parents' expectations for high quality
	30 hours free entitlement	
	Changes to funding for childcare qualifications	

Technological	Legal	Environmental
Parents' expectations – online booking, e-invoices, social media updates etc.	DBS checks for wider group	Climate change – flooding risk in local area
Gov't departments expect electronic communications	Regulation changes with regards to Paediatric First Aid and Food Safety and Allergens	School expansion resulting in builders on site – safeguarding concerns
Changes to equipment and software updates required	Employment law changes following BREXIT	Proposed bus route changes affecting village – drop in numbers and eventual closure
E-safety risks – viruses, hackers etc.		Cost of nappy disposal
Staff training on new systems		

Tips for completing a PESTLE Analysis

- Do plenty of research beforehand and continue to do this on an ongoing basis.

- Get other people with different perspectives and areas of interest involved.

- Think about how to keep it up to date – read business press, but also take advantage of easy ways of gaining information, e.g., e-newsletters, Twitter.

- Avoid navel gazing. Focus your attention outside of the early years sector – don't only think about forthcoming legal changes in childcare, think about forthcoming legal changes affecting small businesses, employment law, etc.

- Don't be afraid to leave it for a while – go away and research some more, then come back and add to it.

7S Analysis – structured navel gazing

The McKinsey 7S model was devised by Tom Peters and Robert H. Waterman Jnr to underpin the thinking in their 1982 book *In Search of Excellence.*

The use of a 7S Analysis will help you to review the internal effectiveness of your early years business and can be especially useful when you have decided on a change in strategy/approach that you want to implement. When used in this scenario it can help to make sure all elements of the business, e.g. numbers of staff, systems and processes, premises, are fit for purpose (strategically aligned) for the future. All the elements of the model are interlinked, just as all elements of your business are linked. If you change one of them, they all need to be changed. So in a change management situation it indicates that you need to give proper consideration to ALL of the elements and not just the one that you wish to change. An example of this would be where a setting decides to change its opening hours. This strategic change impacts on each of the elements within the model.

How to use a 7S Analysis

Using each of the headings, brainstorm what is in place in your setting at the moment, as it is now. Then think about the changes you wish to introduce in the future and go through each of the headings again noting any elements where what needs to be in place in the future differs from what is there at the moment. Finally define the nature of the gaps. Here are some questions to prompt your thinking:

SHARED VALUES

- What are our core values?

- Are they well defined or just something we have thought about?

- How well are they communicated/embedded in everything that we do?

- Does every member of our team care about those values as much as we do?

- If our business were a stick of rock, what is the key message that you'd see running all the way through it?

STRATEGY

- Do we have a clear and well defined strategy for the business?

- Is it written down?

- How well is it communicated and used to provide direction for everything that we do?

- Is it reviewed at least annually to ensure it remains current in the light of changes affecting the sector?

STRUCTURE

- Are our premises fit for purpose?

- Do they meet our current and future needs, providing us with the flexibility to change how we operate?

- Do we have sufficient high quality equipment to provide a rich enabling environment for the children?

SYSTEMS

- What are the main systems and processes that we use to run the business (consider paper-based and informal as well as IT-based systems)?

- How effectively do our systems and processes operate? And how do we know?

- Could any of our systems and processes be improved?

STAFF

- How is our team structured?

- What are the key specialist roles within the team?

- How do we succession plan for the future?

- Do we have the right number of staff to meet ratio requirements, to deliver high quality childcare and to ensure we operate sustainably?

SKILLS

- What skills are essential to enable us to operate effectively (consider qualification requirements as well)?

- Do we have any gaps?

- Do we have a development plan in place to ensure we build the skills we will need in the future?

STYLE

- How participative is our management style?

- How would staff, parents and children describe 'the feel' of our setting?

- How well do team members cooperate and collaborate to get the job done?

When you are planning a change it's really useful to complete the 7S Analysis twice – once showing how things are now and then again showing how things need to be in the future to support your plans for change. Once you've done this you will be able to see where you are already in good shape for the future (your strengths) and where you need to make either minor tweaks or major changes in order to deliver your future plans (your weaknesses).

Strategy	Structure	Systems
Clear strategy to gradually grow a small chain of day nurseries within close proximity, suitable for working parents that live locally and commute, offer a high ratio of staff to children, all food, nappies, wipes etc. included in the cost so parents don't need to worry about them	Own premises or long lease, space to allow expansion (except Setting A), layout allows freeflow including outdoors, equipment maintained to high standard	Strong: payroll, collecting fees, invoicing, EYFS tracking, Ofsted SEF, recruitment, performance management, finance systems, policies and procedures in place and up to date Weak: marketing, building relationships with parents

	Shared values	
	Company vision and ethos is clear in owner's mind but not well understood by staff	

Style	Skills	Staff
To create a home from home environment for the children, especially those accessing full day care Involvement of junior staff in key projects – not yet effective, often causes confusion	95% of staff qualified to Level 2 or higher, only one apprentice in each nursery, a range of different skills at management level, one director holds a degree in HR and the other in Early Childhood studies. In house and external training provided to support CPD, training plan in place	A tiered management system is well established, no long term vacancies, bank staff used to cover sickness and holiday, no agency staff are ever used, staff from various cultures which helps to promote diversity, flexible working currently being discussed

Tips for completing a 7S Analysis

- Get other people with different perspectives and areas of interest involved.

- Be really honest about whether what is in place currently is right to support the setting's future needs and plans but avoid being overly critical – it's important to recognise and acknowledge what's working well, or what has the potential to work well, to avoid throwing out the baby with the bathwater.

- Think about how to keep it up to date as changes are made.

- Don't be afraid to leave it for a while, go away and do some more research then come back and add to your analysis.

Stakeholder Analysis

This tool helps you to consider the points of view of various stakeholders. I would define a stakeholder as being any person or organisation that has an interest in what your early years business does or is in some way affected by it. Stakeholders in your early years business might include local schools, parents, staff, Ofsted, competitors, partners, the local authority, etc. Stakeholder Analysis allows you to determine how best to communicate with each of your stakeholders in order to gain their support for and co-operation with any plans that you have for the future.

How to use a Stakeholder Analysis

Think about a change that you are planning to make in your setting. Begin by making a list of all your stakeholders, both internal and external. Be as specific as possible – so, for example, rather than simply mentioning staff, see if you can identify specific staff members who might feel differently about your plans.

Then decide where you think they are on the Commitment Ladder. Here each of the rungs of the ladder is explained:

- *Fans* – these are the people who are 100 per cent on board with your plans; they want to be involved in making things happen; they're prepared to roll up their sleeves and get their hands dirty; they are happy to tell everyone else how great the plans are.

- *Passive advocates* – these people are generally supportive of your plans but are quite cautious in their support; may be reluctant to go out of their way to make things happen.

- *What's in it for me?* – these people are sitting firmly on the fence and are waiting for you to sell your ideas to them in a way that enables them to see how your plans will be of personal benefit to them.

- *Passive resistors* – these people don't really agree with your plans and are most likely to hold things back by doing nothing, by dragging their heels, by going back to how they've always done things and by generally hindering the progress of change; they may not speak out about their opposition to your plans leaving you believing that they are actually in favour.

- *Well poisoners* – these are the people who whisper in corners about what a bad idea they think this is; they are good at building alliances and gathering supporters around them and can easily infect passive resistors and what's in it for me? people with their negativity.

- *Saboteurs* – these are the people who will openly object to your plans and who will go out of their way to prevent those plans from being implemented.

Next, consider how much influence over others each stakeholder might have. Do they have the power or authority to make or break your plans, or are they people you can work around?

Using the matrix template in Appendix 4, put all of your stakeholders in the right place depending on their level of influence and where they are on the commitment ladder. So, someone who is a fan but hasn't much influence would be at the top but in the middle (from left to right), someone who is a passive resistor but has lots of influence would be in the middle on the vertical scale, but right over towards the right hand side.

Once you've added all your stakeholders onto the matrix start to consider what your communication strategy for each group might be.

- Those towards the top right, i.e. highly committed to your plans and influential – consider giving them lead roles or asking them to advocate on your behalf to influence less committed stakeholders; if you have no one in this area, you might find that you struggle to implement your plans.

- Those towards the top left, i.e. highly committed but with low influence – consider ways in which you might extend their influence, for example by making them change champions and encouraging them to talk to others about how they feel or by giving them a role to play.

- Those towards the bottom right, i.e. negative towards your plans but highly influential – if you can't win them over, consider how to prevent them from negatively influencing others; often these people end up isolating themselves as support grows amongst other people.

- Those towards the bottom left, i.e. neither committed nor influential – don't waste too much time on them but keep an eye on them in case they become more influential.

High		
LA EY team	Working parents	School business manager EY manager
	Local childminding group Staff already on flexible contracts	Committee
		Governing board
Non-working parents The children		Executive principal
	Neighbours	
Low	Caretaker Staff still on full time contracts	

COMMITMENT

Low   **INFLUENCE**   **High**

Tips for completing a Stakeholder Analysis

- Think widely about all internal and external stakeholders – anyone who has an interest in your setting is a stakeholder.

- Be as specific as possible, breaking down large groups of people into smaller chunks, e.g. some staff may be supportive whilst other are not.

- Think about relationships between stakeholders and how you might make use of these to influence some of your stakeholders.

- Review your Stakeholder Analysis from time to time as people may well move as your plans evolve.

- Treat this information sensitively – this isn't the sort of thing to stick up on the wall or to circulate widely as some people may be offended to see where you have placed them on the matrix.

Market Analysis

Local authorities have a duty to ensure sufficient childcare places are available in their areas to meet the needs of local families. Many conduct Childcare Sufficiency Studies and report on this. Accessing these reports can be a valuable starting place for an early years business trying to predict future need for services and planning to offer places to meet that need. You can also access data about birth rates.

The problem, however, is that in recent years, with cuts to local authority funding, many have not kept this data up to date. In some cases these reports may be four or five years old and may not take account of things like house building plans approved in more recent years. You will also find that these reports are quite general in nature and don't provide the level of highly localised information that you may need in order to plan properly.

So, it really is down to you to do your own assessment of likely parental demand for childcare in your area. The planning, of course, becomes even more challenging if the families you tend to attract don't live in your immediate area but work locally, or pass your setting on their way to work. And with the introduction of the 30 hours offer, you will also need to gauge the needs of working parents who are likely to want to access that service.

A good Market Analysis should also include researching your competitors.

Conducting parental research

Many early years businesses conduct market research with their current customers. This works fine if your plans involve finding out how your existing customers feel about your services, or if you are planning to offer something different to your existing customers, for example, longer opening hours. It is also useful if your plans include finding additional customers who are similar to your existing ones.

However, this is not so useful if you need to find out about the needs of parents who are not currently using your services. An example of this would be a school nursery that currently offers term time only care during school hours. If the setting is thinking of expanding to take advantage of the 30 hours offer they need to be talking to working parents who are probably not currently using their services to find out what their needs are.

Accessing these parents may need some more creative forms of market research, perhaps involving current customers introducing you to their friends, neighbours or work colleagues, or using social media. Or, if you live in a commuter town, surveying parents on their way to/from work.

So, thinking about the sort of customers you need to research is your first step – is it the same customers you already have or different ones?

Conducting competitor research

All businesses have a need to understand how they compare with others. Knowing this will help you to develop marketing messages that clearly differentiate your business and what you offer from all the rest.

Some ways that you might consider conducting competitor research include:

- Website review – many early years businesses share a lot of information on their publicly accessible websites, not thinking that many of the people who take a look at this information might well be their competitors. Check out what your competitors say about themselves on their website – what sort of impression do they make, and how does this compare with your business?

- Asking others – if you interview a prospective staff member or meet a prospective customer, ask them which other settings they have been to see and what they thought about them.

- Mystery shopping – this involves calling up a competitor (and maybe arranging to visit if they don't know you) as if you were a prospective customer. I did know one setting owner who, when considering opening a baby room, borrowed her sister's baby and visited various competitors to review their baby rooms.

- Being open about the fact that you are doing market research – if this is done in the spirit of reciprocation (I'll show you mine if you show me yours), some competitors may be quite open about sharing information with you or even allowing you to visit their setting to have a look around.

Top tips for using surveys and questionnaires as part of a Market Analysis

Surveys and questionnaires are very useful when conducting market research – here are a few tips for effective use of surveys and questionnaires:

- Don't ask for information that you don't need – for each question think in advance about what you really want to find out and what use you will make of that information.

- Don't make it too long.

- Make it simple to complete – tick boxes and multiple choice questions are quick and easy for people to fill in.

- If you have the opportunity to meet respondents face to face, complete it for/with them (a school I work with massively increased parental responses to their surveys by asking governors to hand the questionnaires out to parents while they were waiting for appointments with staff at parent consultation evenings).

- Include a couple of sections where people can write in their answer in case they have something that they really want to say.

- Allow people to complete it anonymously but collect some information about them, e.g. where they live, ages of children, working patterns, etc. (again only collect information that is useful and relevant).

- Consider using free online tools such as SurveyMonkey if you have email addresses for possible respondents or if you have a substantial following on your Facebook page.

- When you have completed the survey and analysed the results be prepared to share some of what you've found out, especially if you asked existing customers to complete it. Some settings report back with a section in their newsletter saying 'You said this – so we're doing this' – this builds your credibility by showing that you are listening.

Pulling it all together

This section covers how to make use of the results of the various pieces of business analysis undertaken to inform decisions about the future of your early years business. I like to use a SWOT Analysis to do this.

The results of your PESTLE Analysis can be used to populate the Opportunities and Threats sections of your SWOT Analysis. To do this, go through the points you've identified in your PESTLE Analysis and pick out those that represent great opportunities for your setting for the future. Then pick out those points that represent significant threats – those that are most likely to happen and which will also have a significant negative impact on your setting if/when they do.

With your 7S Analysis, identify those elements where your business is already in great shape for the future. Add those points to the Strengths area of your SWOT Analysis. Then identify those where you found gaps between how things are now and how you need them to be in the future. Add these to your Weaknesses box.

Do the same with your Stakeholder Analysis, adding influential supporters to your Strengths and influential resistors to your Weaknesses.

Then identify those aspects of your Market Analysis that represent Opportunities to deliver something that parents want and that your competitors don't offer, and those that represent Threats, and add those to your SWOT Analysis as well.

Finally continue to build your SWOT Analysis by including your conclusions from other analyses, such as financial forecasting and training needs analysis, suggested throughout this book.

Making things happen

I sometimes get people on my courses who say, 'Oh yes we've completed a SWOT before – it wasn't very useful', but when I ask what they did with it, they actually stopped at this point, in which case it's no more than a time consuming exercise in navel gazing. Your next step has to be to ask yourself what you need to do in order to:

- build on and protect your strengths

- eliminate or improve your weaknesses

- take advantage of the opportunities

- reduce the negative impact of the threats.

It is often helpful to try to quantify the nature of the points you have added to your SWOT Analysis. Some will be really significant weaknesses or threats that may actually be insurmountable, whilst others may be things that you can overcome or improve quite easily.

Some opportunities may be easier to take advantage of than others and more likely to come about.

This way the SWOT Analysis, the methodology I've recommended, and the tools that fed information into it, becomes a valuable tool for driving business improvement and for underpinning your plans to implement change. Use the points you've included in your SWOT Analysis to help you to define your key performance indicators (KPIs) and targets in your early years business dashboard.

If you are ever in a position of seeking support for your plans from others (governors and trustees, or funders maybe), this will provide an excellent demonstration of the in-depth and robust analysis that you've undertaken to justify your arguments.

Finally, in order to turn this into a meaningful action plan, I recommend that you focus on the step you need to take now to get things started. How will that first step be taken, when and by whom? And you're on your way to building your early years business.

Chapter 3

OPTIONS FOR STRUCTURING YOUR EARLY YEARS BUSINESS

This chapter covers some of the basic considerations about possible legal structures for your early years business, but doesn't attempt to duplicate much more extensive existing publications such as Playwork Partnership's excellent *Getting It Right Legally* publication (University of Gloucestershire and Bates, Wells and Braithwaite London LLP 2013). I must also stress that a book like this can't possibly provide legal advice. It highlights some considerations that you should think about before seeking legal advice to help you to make the right decisions.

What are my options?

One of the first decisions you will need to make when starting up your early years business is what kind of legal structure (or legal entity) you should opt for. This is an important decision to make as it has implications affecting matters such as:

- how you and your business will be taxed

- how easy it will be for you to attract funding

- how to grow your business

- who is legally liable if thing go wrong

- how to dispose of your business when you no longer wish to run it (such as when you retire).

Although it is possible to change your legal structure at a later date, this is costly and in some cases complicated. So, it is a bit like making the decision to get married – take time to get it right in the first place to avoid a costly and messy divorce at a later date.

The basic options that are available to you are set out in the table below:

Legal structure	What does this mean?
Sole trader	Means that you and your business are one and the same and that you are personally registered with HMRC e.g. Jane Brown Trading As ABC Day Nursery – often referred to as 'being self-employed'
Partnership	Means you have a formal agreement in place with one or more other people to own and run the business – responsibilities, investment and profits are shared as set out in the Partnership Agreement
Limited Company	Means that you have set up a separate legal entity registered with Companies House and that you are a shareholder and can benefit personally from any profit generated (you may also be employed as a Director)
Registered Charity	Means that you have registered your organisation with the Charity Commission and that all profits (known as a surplus) are used to further the organisation's charitable objectives – can be either unincorporated or a Charitable Incorporated Organisation (or CIO) – managed by a board of trustees (known as a voluntary management committee in our sector) – may be limited by shares or by guarantee
Community Interest Company (CIC)	Means that your business is registered with the Registrar of Community Interest Companies as having a primarily social objective – often referred to as a social enterprise; the use of a 'Dividend Cap' strikes a balance between encouraging people to invest in a CIC and the principle that assets and profits should be devoted to the benefit of the community
Co-operative	Means the business is owned by members, such as staff (as in the John Lewis model) or customers (as in the Co-operative model), and may have a number of different legal structures

There are pros and cons relating to each of these options and I'm going to outline some of these, with specific reference to the factors that an early years business might need to take into account. And there are many other factors to weigh up, such as where your main source of income comes from: fees, investors, grant/trust funding, donations, etc., as these may be limited by certain legal structures.

Legal status decision map

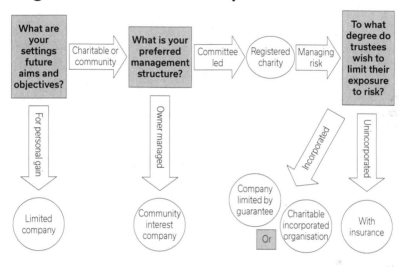

Legal structure	Advantages for an EY business	Disadvantages for an EY business
Sole trader	• Can be cheaper to run than incorporated businesses • Do not need to submit audited accounts • Provide very limited information publicly • Lower accountancy fees	• Has no legal identity separate from its members so all property, contracts and leases required by the business are owned by the sole trader personally • Carries personal unlimited liability so personal assets can be seized to settle the debts of the business • Sole trader is taxed on business income at his/her top marginal rate of income tax
Partnership	• Ideal when two or more people share common purposes and wish to go into business together, with rules to identify how it works • Easy to establish • Can obtain limited liability (solicitors often use this structure operating as Limited Liability Partnerships LLPs) • No formal public Annual Return required – each partner is taxed personally on their share of the profit • Partnerships are liable for VAT and capital gains tax (CGT) • Little regulation to deal with	• Has no legal identity separate from its members so all property, contracts and leases required by the business must be owned by one or more of the partners as individuals • Partners carry personal unlimited liability for the organisation's debts including for decisions taken by other partners (partners are jointly and severally responsible for the debts of the partnership) so a partner's personal assets can be seized to settle the partnership's debts • Each partner can make decisions and enter contracts without prior approval of other partners • Problems if partner wishes to leave or if a partner dies may lead to the automatic dissolution of the partnership • Potential for personality conflicts

| Limited Company | • Enables members and owners to minimise their liabilities through the creation of a separate legal entity; the business is the legal entity that enters into contracts, employs staff, leases property etc. – without incorporation it is the individuals, e.g. trustees themselves, who personally do these things

• Company Limited by Guarantee (CLG) differs from the more common Company Limited by Shares in that it does not have shareholders (members merely guarantee a nominal contribution to its assets should it become insolvent)

• Can be operated alongside a registered charity

• Easy and quick to set up – off the shelf companies can be used – requiring only one member

• Little capital required at start

• Low registration costs

• Provides formalised governance within a legal framework which can increase public confidence (many banks and financial institutions will insist on incorporation before providing loan finance)

• Highly flexible – a broad range of constitutional arrangements can be adopted, including co-operative type constitutions

• Directors can be paid

• The business can continue if one or more members leave | • Wide body of legislation must be adhered to – regulations are not designed with social enterprises in mind

• Full tax, National Insurance and corporate rates apply unless charitable status also obtained (this would entail dual registration with Companies House and the Charity Commission with two sets of paperwork to complete) which may lead to higher accountancy costs

• Capital cannot be raised through share issues and banks often don't like lending to CLGs because they have limited assets

• Must submit a set of audited accounts and an annual return (known as a Confirmation Statement), which are publicly available, exposing the enterprise to scrutiny by competitors

• People can view a company structure as being synonymous with a profit orientation

• In a charity that also operates as a limited company, Trustees are also listed as Directors. Directors have a personal responsibility to ensure statutory documents are delivered to Companies House when required, with fines for non-compliance:
– Annual accounts
– Confirmation Statement, which includes:
  – Notice of change of directors and their contact details
  – Notice of change of registered office |

Legal structure	Advantages for an EY business	Disadvantages for an EY business
Registered Charity	• Can lend organisation 'legitimacy' • Is a prerequisite for some donors and funding bodies to offer support • Helpful for fundraising • Removes the tax burden on the organisation, e.g. exemption from corporation tax, certain VAT relief, exemption from stamp duty on conveyancing, reduced business rates on premises • Donors can receive tax relief on donations • A Charitable Incorporated Organisation (or CIO) is an incorporated form of charity which is not a company – this provides limited liability for trustees and may be simpler than establishing a charitable company as avoids dual registration (so suitable for small organisations which employ staff and/or enter into contracts)	• Takes time to be granted by the Charity Commissioners • Some charitable structures do not provide trustees with limited liability • The requirement to operate with a board of trustees (voluntary management committee) can prove to be challenging – charitable status means trustees can't normally be paid therefore limiting the skilled professional input available • Restricts permissible trading activities • All assets are held in trust and can't be sold, making transfer of ownership difficult • Altering trust deeds (constitutions) can be complicated

Community Interest Company (CIC)	• Low registration costs • CIC regulations designed to serve community enterprises rather than personal and private gain and ideal for smaller organisations • Limited liability for directors • Dividends can be paid in line with the specific constitution of the CIC and so can encourage investors • Can continue if one or more members leave as the company is 'controlled' by the members, who appoint directors to govern the enterprise • May still be eligible for grant funding • Some structures provide a way for allowing other people such as staff to take shares in the business, giving a sense of ownership	• An 'asset lock' ensures that the assets of the CIC, including any profits are used for the community purposes for which it was formed or transferred to another asset-locked organisation – these rules are quite complicated • Free to operate more commercially than a registered charity but doesn't have the same tax advantages, e.g. Gift Aid • Must submit a set of audited accounts and an annual return which are publicly available – this exposes the enterprise to scrutiny by competitors • The asset lock and dividend cap may deter investors and deter banks from lending • Full tax, NI and corporate rates apply • The 'asset lock' means members cannot amend the constitution and benefit from the disposal of assets
Co-operative	• The primary objective is to benefit its members, through access to goods and services provided by the co-operative • The benefit members receive is in proportion to their level or participation in the co-operative • A business form that offers a democratic way for stakeholders to participate as equal partners	• Not clearly defined in English Law but governed by the co-operative principles as prescribed by the International Co-operative Association (ICA) • Profits belong to its members, to be used solely for the benefit of members, or for the wider community • Because surplus profits can be distributed to members (no asset lock), co-operatives are regarded as being closer to the private sector than charity, so they are often less likely to be able to gain access to charitable grants or donations

Organisational registration

Owners and trustees must ensure that the business is registered, as required by law, with various organisations, depending on your legal structure: Ofsted, of course, but also the Charity Commission and/or Companies House and/or other bodies such as the Registrar of Companies (if it is a company limited by guarantee or by shares) or the Registrar of CICs (if it is a Community Interest Company) and Her Majesty's Revenue & Customs (HMRC – 'the taxman').

It staggers me that I am still coming across settings who are operating on an informal basis as unincorporated associations or 'clubs' and are in breach of so many pieces of legislation that I can hardly begin to list them all.

You should make sure that you have a clear understanding of the legal obligations that your registration places on you as a business owner or trustee. This will include ensuring that annual reports and accounts are published, and that information is shared with these various bodies as required and in compliance with deadline dates. Because directors and trustees hold a legal obligation, their names and contact details must be recorded with these organisations and this list must be kept up to date. Fines and penalties can be levied for failure to do so.

Changing your legal status

Making a change to an existing legal structure can be complicated and costly, so getting it right in the first place is important. However, if, having read through this chapter so far, you have begun to realise that your current legal structure is not fit for purpose, don't despair – changes can be made. But, if you do decide to go down this route, make sure that you take good advice and budget for the costs and time involved in dealing with matters like TUPE (Transfer of Undertakings (Protection of Employment) Regulations 1981 – the legislation that dictates the way in which staff rights are protected when they are transferred from one employer to another), new Ofsted registration (may currently not be desirable if your setting is graded Outstanding as it would start from scratch again), new contracts with suppliers, legal registration, closing existing business accounts, etc.

The main reasons that I come across for early years businesses to go down this route are where they are currently operating as

Registered Charities and are concerned about the lack of limited liability for owners and/or committee members and/or difficulties experienced in operating with an effective committee. Resolving either of these issues could involve making changes to the legal structure of the setting.

Committee issues can more simply be addressed by changing your constitution to allow recruitment of committee members from a wider pool than your current constitution allows. This may be preferable to changing the legal status of the business so that no committee is required. However, any decisions to change the constitution can only be made by the committee itself. I have come across setting managers who think that they can make the decision to change the constitution or even to disband the committee – they can't.

Advance planning and preparation

I've been supporting a client who is facing a TUPE situation as a result of changing the legal structure of her early years business from a sole trader to a limited company. She was hoping to introduce a couple of clauses into staff contracts to allow for greater flexibility in the future and was disappointed when I indicated that these clauses would be viewed as changes to terms and conditions and so not permitted under TUPE. This situation reminded me of the importance of reviewing contracts of employment regularly and not just at times when a major change is taking place. It would probably have been quite straightforward for her to negotiate the desired changes if she had done so six months earlier, before any plans to transfer staff had been made. Once TUPE applies, employers face significant restrictions.

This is just one example where proper planning and preparation would have been helpful and might have avoided the difficulties they subsequently experienced.

The following checklist has been drawn up by the Charity Commission to assist any charity that is thinking about changing its legal status (I have adapted it so that it can be applied to any setting thinking about changing its legal status):

When you plan the restructure	
Agree purpose of your business	Discuss your business purpose (e.g. to generate a profit for the business owners, community or charitable purpose) and update if necessary.
Choose the right structure	Discuss the types of structure and choose the right structure for your business.
Decide how any assets will transfer	Check that your current governing document allows you to transfer your existing assets to a new business – these rules are likely to be in its dissolution clause. If it doesn't, you may need the Charity Commission or another body to approve the transfer. This will be the case if you operate using the Pre-school Learning Alliance constitution.
Make sure your business is up to date with admin and filing	Make sure your most recent annual return and accounts have been submitted (if applicable). Resolve any outstanding issues raised.
Decide if you need to take legal advice	Take professional advice if you need it to plan your restructure, or consult your umbrella body if you have one. Consult with other bodies e.g. Ofsted
When you apply to register the new business	
Complete the registration process thoroughly	A new charity or business cannot be registered using incomplete applications, so you may need to make decisions before completing the paperwork about directors, shareholders, trustees, etc.
If registering a new charity	Say that the new charity is replacing an existing one and tell the commission about any changes to your charitable purpose objects and your reasons for making them.
Give details of any assets that will transfer and how	Explain which assets will transfer, the powers you have to do this and any approvals you've had to get. This is particularly important for permanent endowment – an asset with conditions on how it can be used.
After your new business is registered	
Transfer any assets and liabilities	Make arrangements to transfer the original assets and liabilities, and staff to the new business, as planned.
Close the original business	Close the original business in line with the rules set out in its governing document. Remove it from the register of charities or other registers.

Effective governance

Whichever legal structure you have decided to implement, you should also think about your governance arrangements. Often we associate the concept of governance with schools, but governance is something that is present in all businesses and organisations.

Getting governance right is important as many business failures and scandals can often be associated with poor governance. Here are a few examples that have made the headlines:

- *Kids Company* – received more than £42M from governments; closed down in 2015 following allegations of sexual abuse on the same day that £3M went into account. Subsequent inquiries found that the primary responsibility for the collapse rested with the trustees, who repeatedly ignored auditors' warnings of precarious finances. It was found that trustees lacked knowledge and experience in the field to enable them to interrogate decisions and lacked a proper attitude towards responsible governance.[1]

- *The Co-operative Group* – the inquiry report called it 'a calamitous failure of governance' and reported that people without the required skills held positions of responsibility and were unable to hold senior management to account or to provide guidance, also that members were elected from a non-democratic clique.[2]

- *Mid Staffordshire NHS Trust* – the 2010 review into standards highlighted many findings that were linked to governance, such as a corporate focus on process rather than outcomes, failure to listen to stakeholders (poor complaints management), lack of continuous professional development

---

1   The Public Administration and Constitutional Affairs Committee appointed by the House of Commons (2016) The collapse of Kids Company: lessons for charity trustees, professional firms, the Charity Commission, and Whitehall. Details available at   www.publications.parliament.uk/pa/cm201516/cmselect/cmpubadm/433/433.pdf accessed on 11 December 2016.

2   Kelly, Sir C. (2014) 'Failings in management and governance Report of the independent review into the events leading to the Co-operative Bank's capital shortfall.' Details available at www.coop.co.uk/corporate/the-kelly-review accessed on 11 December 2016.

(CPD) and appraisal and lack of overview of policies and procedures.[3]

- *'Trojan Horse' Inquiry* – the government inquiry uncovered an organised attempt by a number of associated individuals to introduce an extreme Islamist ethos into several schools in Birmingham, with plans to extend this to other cities. This was achieved by appointing those individuals and their family members to governance roles within various schools.[4]

- *VW* – the diesel emissions scandal in 2015 resulted in billions of dollars of compensation being paid out and millions of cars being recalled. Management admitted that software had been fitted to 11 million cars with the intention of duping emission tests and apologised. Senior appointments causing 'serious conflicts of interest' were cited as an example of VW's 'uniquely awful governance'.[5]

- *Sports Direct* – when appalling illegal employment practices were uncovered, owner Mike Ashley admitted that the business had 'perhaps grown too big for him to manage'. The lack of independent directors led to serious concerns about corporate governance and oversight.[6]

- *BHS* – the Parliamentary review found that leadership failures and greed led to the failure of the High Street brand with 'egregious failures of corporate governance' being cited as contributing to the failure of the retail business and the disastrous state of the employees' pensions scheme.[7]

---

3   The Mid Staffordshire NHS Foundation Trust Public Inquiry (2013). Details available at http://www.midstaffspublicinquiry.com accessed on 11 December 2016.

4   Clarke, P. CVO OBE QPM (July 2014) Report into allegations concerning Birmingham schools arising from the 'Trojan Horse' letter. Details available at www.gov.uk/government/publications/birmingham-schools-education-commissioners-report accessed on 11 December 2016.

5   Bryant, C. and Milne, R. (2015) 'Boardroom politics at heart of VW scandal.' *Financial Times*, 4 October.

6   Torrance, J. (June 2016) 'Has Sports Direct grown too big for Mike Ashley to handle?' *Management Today*, June. Details available at www.managementtoday.co.uk/sports-direct-grown-big-mike-ashley-handle/leadership-lessons/article/1397891 accessed on 11 December 2016.

7   Business, Innovation and Skills and Work and Pensions Committees (25 July 2016) The sale and acquisition of BHS inquiry, HC 54. London: House of Commons.

So what is meant by the term governance? And how can good governance be achieved in an early years business? First it's important to differentiate between management and governance.

Management is about:

- running the setting on a day to day basis

- making operational decisions (short term, minor details, day to day, business as usual, etc.)

- dealing with the children, staff and parents.

Governance is about:

- overseeing what happens in the setting to ensure good standards are maintained and that children are kept safe

- making strategic decisions (long term, big picture, significant change, etc.)

- monitoring how the setting deals with children, staff and parents.

Some suggested governance structures that might be suitable for an early years business include:

- If your business is a charity you must have a Board of Trustees (often referred to in our sector as a Voluntary Management Committee).

- If your business is a Limited Company – appointing non-executive directors (NEDs) is a great way of ensuring governance and bringing additional skills into your business at a senior level.

- If your business has another legal structure – consider creating an Advisory Board with individuals appointed who can support, advise and challenge senior management.

Whatever the legal status of your business, parent-led consultation committees and other groups can be very beneficial, including advisory boards, partnership boards and staff consultation committees.

The role of trustees, committee members, non-executive directors and governors is to monitor whether things are being done rather than to do them themselves. Monitoring of this sort is a key expectation of Ofsted and of other bodies and involves:

- asking for regular reports from senior staff

- confirming that appropriate policies and procedures are in place and up to date

- asking challenging questions

- understanding data and other documentation

- visiting the setting to check things out

- making sure that children are safe and well cared for in the setting

- ensuring financial probity and integrity.

It is also a strategic role with a focus on helping the business to put into place a clear vision and to develop a strategic plan to move towards the delivery of that vision.

Tips on developing effective governance

The National Governors Association (NGA) identifies the following as the eight elements of governance for schools and these are equally applicable to any early years business.

Element 1: Getting the right people around the table – ideally you are looking for people who:

- are dedicated to and passionate about the interests and activities of your business

- are committed to high standards of ethics and integrity

- are happy to accept a level of accountability

- bring a balance/mix of professional skills

- you know and trust.

If it is mandatory for you to operate with a board of trustees, you should put into place a rolling programme of recruitment (don't wait until committee members have resigned before you start looking for new ones).

Element 2: Developing their understanding of their roles and responsibilities – once you have appointed suitable people you should also make sure that they understand their roles and responsibilities by:

- defining roles and responsibilities (see the checklist below)

- making your expectations clear by introducing a code of conduct

- considering gaps in knowledge and skills and how these might be filled through training or further recruitment

- putting into place training and development for all committee members especially those in key roles (chair, treasurer, secretary) and those with key responsibilities (marketing, staff management, health and safety)

- organising the work of the committee ensuring duties are widely spread.

People in governance roles are expected to fulfil a number of key roles. These are equally applicable to any individuals fulfilling a governance role regardless of your legal structure. The National Council of Voluntary Organisations (NCVO) provides a useful checklist which I have adapted here:

1. Define the organisation's vision (what we want to be like), mission (what sort of organisation are we) and values (what matters to us).

2. Develop a strategy designed to deliver the vision and in line with the mission and values.

3. Establish and monitor policies and procedures.

4. Ensure compliance with governing document/constitution.

5. Ensure compliance with the law.

6. Exercise financial oversight.

7. Recruit, manage and support senior managers.

8. Respect the role of staff by avoiding trying to do their job for them.

9. Self assess your own performance as a committee or governance team and take steps to develop effectiveness.

10. Champion and promote the organisation to the outside world.

Element 3: Electing an effective Chair who has the skills to fulfil this important role effectively – this is likely to mean that you need to provide training for that individual. It is also important to succession plan for their replacement.

Element 4: Having a clerk or secretary to your board, who can provide advice about your legal obligations, to keep you on the straight and narrow.

Element 5: Good relationships built on trust – maybe it goes without saying but I find myself working with many settings where relationships between the committee/board and senior management have broken down or where there is conflict within the committee itself that prevents them from operating effectively. Elements 1–3 above can help you to ensure your relationships are built on trust.

Element 6: Knowing your setting – this means having a real understanding of the setting, staff, children, performance data, the local community, etc. Making this work relies on good information being shared by the leadership team and a commitment from committee members or trustees to visit and find out how things work on a day to day basis.

Element 7: Being committed to asking challenging questions – a committee or board that simply sits and nods in agreement to whatever they are being told by management is of no value whatsoever. Making sure that members of the board have the skills to ask challenging questions in an appropriate way is essential.

Element 8: Having the confidence to have courageous conversations – as well as having the competence to ask challenging questions, committee members and trustees must also have the confidence to do so in the best interest of the children at the setting.

You might also find the following checklist helpful to work through:

Does your early years business:	Yes/ no	If no – we need to:
Have an appropriate legal structure		Check what would be involved in making a change
Have a governing document that sets out who currently fulfils governance roles (trustees, committee, governing body, etc.)		Write a constitution, terms of reference etc.

Have the right people in governance roles		Complete a skills audit considering the skills, knowledge and experience that you need and what you have already – plan to recruit new people with the knowledge and skills you need or provide training to existing members
Ensure all those in governance roles understand their roles and responsibilities		Provide role descriptions and a code of conduct, and plan training
Ensure all those in governance roles have access to appropriate independent advice		Join organisations that can advise you, attend their meetings and events, look on their websites, sign up to e-newsletters
Have a clear vision for the future that describes how you would like the business to be		Describe your vision for the future, both in terms of your childcare provision and in terms of your business
Ensure all reports and returns that need to be published for your business are lodged on time		Create a annual timetable showing when these returns are due
Have a whistle-blowing policy that sets out who those in governance roles should tell if they have any concerns		Develop a whistle-blowing policy and ensure it is communicated with everyone
Have people in governance roles who know what's going on in your setting and have the authority to ask challenging questions to ensure compliance		Encourage them to visit the setting and ask questions to find out more about things like vision and ethos, performance data, policies and procedures, curriculum, finances, parents, children and staff, etc.
Have a governance structure where everyone has a part to play		Organise the work of those in governance roles so that everyone plays a part (you might like to allocate lead roles such as safeguarding, marketing, finance, fundraising, staffing etc.)
Have a regular programme of monitoring key areas of risk and key aspects of your Early Years Business Dashboard		Agree a monitoring programme annually

Chapter 4

FINANCIAL MANAGEMENT

The financial challenges faced by early years businesses are significant but not insurmountable; the introduction of the 30 hours offer for working parents means for many an increase in the number of funded hours that they offer, with a similar reduction in hours paid for by parents; rules affecting how extra costs can be passed onto parents are a restriction. Ensuring the long term sustainability of your business means developing excellent financial management skills and being prepared to both work innovatively and to take tough decisions.

Good practice in relation to financial management will both help you to manage your business, ensuring that it is operating on a sustainable footing, whilst at the same time ensuring compliance with the tax man's expectations. So this chapter addresses some of the issues that you will need to consider as a part of the finance section of your Early Years Business Dashboard.

Funding strategy

The first step in managing your finances is to set out clearly how you expect to generate income to operate your early years business. This is called a funding strategy.

A well thought through funding strategy should be driven by your vision for the future and your overall business strategy. So, for example, if your overall business strategy is to build a profitable business which you can then sell to fund your retirement, then a funding strategy built on a charitable model is not going to be suitable. If your business strategy is all about serving current and future generations of children in your local community then your funding strategy needs to be built on ensuring the long term sustainability of the business with profits being reinvested into the business to develop and sustain its assets.

Your funding strategy should clearly show:

- where your income will come from, for example, Free Early Education Entitlement Funding (FEEE), fees, Early Years Pupil Premium (EYPP), grants, loans, rental etc.

- how much of your income will come from each source

- any risks or dependencies relating to each source of income, for example, EYPP being allocated in relation to specific children who may not be with you next year.

Your funding strategy should be set out in writing so that it can be used to demonstrate to external stakeholders such as a bank or other funders that you have a coherent plan, and also to provide continuity within your senior team. This is of particular issue to settings run by a committee of volunteers where membership of the committee changes regularly and where effective handover is sometimes lacking.

As with any strategy, your funding strategy should be reviewed and updated regularly, whenever any changes to your funding sources are announced, such as changes to the free entitlement funding rate or the rate being paid for Early Years Pupil Premium.

Planning for the 30 hours offer

At the time of writing this book, everyone is talking about the government's new offer to provide 30 hours of funded childcare for working parents. Just as when the original 15 hours of universal entitlement was first introduced, this means that you need to do some careful and thorough financial planning to ensure you make informed decisions about how your business will offer this.

First of all, I would recommend that you ignore a lot of the scare-mongering and rumours that are being spread in the trade press and on social media. All the noise and negativity really isn't helpful. And it's essential that you don't base important business decisions on what others might be saying. Your decisions need to be based on what you know about your business. So read the Statutory Guidance thoroughly and make sure that you fully understand the rules and any restrictions that might apply to your business and your parents.

The rules around invoicing often catch people out so confirm with your local authority contacts what you can and can't do.

The usual rules continue to apply with regard to charging for any goods or services (e.g. meals, optional extra activities, additional hours), this must not be made a condition of children accessing a place; the early education places must be delivered completely free of charge to parents. Apart from this, any charges outside the free places are a matter for you to negotiate with parents.

At a recent conference that we ran, Ross Midgley from People and Business Development stressed that providers need to think carefully about the financial impact that offering a funded place will have. This applies to a 15 hour funded place, but even more so when you are considering a 30 hours funded place. Ross provided a useful model to help settings to determine the extent to which they should offer places for funded children.

	OCCUPANCY	
	Low	High
High	Any bookings welcome. Probably more urgent problems than funding shortfall	May consider opting out of free entitlement but need to consider reaction of existing parents to loss of subsidy
FEES		
Low	Any bookings welcome. Funding shortfall non-existent or relatively unimportant	Funding shortfall non-existent or relatively unimportant. 30 hours probably welcome as this reduces the likelihood of funded places interfering with full time paid places

A useful question he encouraged settings to ask themselves when using this model is: 'Will the next funded child you take on add to or reduce your profit?'

The price is right!

Setting the right price for your service and figuring out the impact of taking on funded children is critical if you want both to attract customers and generate a surplus or profit. There are many factors that settings must consider in making these important decisions. This next section runs through a few of those considerations. It's not going to give you the answers for your business but will alert you to the sort of things that you need to be thinking about in order to get this right.

Calculating whether you are breaking even (covering your costs) is the most important factor to take into account when setting a price for your services and also when determining how taking on a funded child for 15 or for 30 hours will impact on your finances, and I'm going to address this later in the chapter. But there are other factors that you should also take into account as well. These are linked very closely to your marketing plan and reflect the kind of setting that you are and the kind of parents you are targeting.

Market positioning

First of all, decide where you want to position yourself in the childcare market. You could, for example, decide that you want to position yourself as a premium-priced provider, charging more than other local settings. There is nothing wrong with making this decision, but as with every business decision, choosing to be the Harrods of local early years carries consequences. If you make this decision you need to ask yourself:

- Can you guarantee that you can at all times provide a premium standard of service to meet your customers' high expectations?

- Are you located in an area where there is a sufficiently large pool of affluent parents to be able to attract enough customers to fill your places?

- How do you feel about potentially excluding some families from using your services?

The expectations of parents in this situation will be to pay more because they believe this means they will receive a higher standard of care for their children. Although we know that this is not necessarily true, working with that perception can be helpful. If your customers are people for whom high quality matters, charging a lower price actually devalues your service. Those parents expect to be able to say to their friends, 'We pay to send Jessica to the XYZ Nursery. It's terribly expensive but awfully good you know.' They may associate paying a higher fee with higher quality provision.

On the other hand, there is nothing wrong with deciding that you want to market your setting as a budget-priced provider, charging towards the lower end of the market or being more reliant on fully funded children. But again making that decision carries consequences. If you make this decision you need to ask yourself:

- Can you generate sufficient income to cover your costs and break even?

- If money is tight, and you need to keep staff costs down, this may mean paying staff at National Living Wage. If so how will you attract and retain quality staff?

- Are you likely to attract families who themselves have financial difficulties? If so what sort of late payment and debt management processes will you need to have in place?

- How will you generate additional money to enable you to invest in the building, equipment, staff training, etc.?

One pricing strategy that I would strongly urge you not to consider is one of being the cheapest provider in your area. This is a dangerous route to follow. Over the years I have seen settings who have set this as their strategy and have then been undercut by a neighbouring setting, causing them to have to cut their prices in order to maintain that strategy. A price war of this sort is ok if you are a big supermarket or a John Lewis, claiming never to be knowingly undersold, but is simply not affordable for a small business. In addition to this, parents who are simply looking for the cheapest childcare they can find may prove to be difficult to engage with and be fickle customers who are quick to move their child if they can find cheaper provision elsewhere. Early years businesses at this end of the market also often report difficulties with bad debt.

Building your understanding of the kind of customers who are likely to use your services is therefore crucial if you want to get your positioning right. I will say more about how to conduct market research in order to do this in Chapter 5.

Whichever decision you make about your positioning you will also need to conduct some competitor research in order to understand what other settings charge. More detail about competitor research is covered in Chapter 5.

Differentiation

It's also useful, when creating your pricing strategy, to think about what it is that you are actually offering and how this sets you apart from your competitors. Early years businesses who offer something that their competitors aren't able to offer, in other words differentiators, are often able to consider charging a premium for those services. Examples of differentiators that you might want to consider include the following factors:

- Your location, e.g. close to the station or the park-and-ride, adjacent to a hospital or other large employer, on a farm, the only setting in a village, etc.

- The hours you are able to offer, e.g. early drop off and late pick up times, overnight or weekend provision to accommodate shift workers, last minute changes requiring flexibility, temporary/emergency childcare, etc.

- The specialist skills that your staff have, e.g. multi-lingual, Forest School trained, skilled at working with children with special needs or severe disabilities, etc.

- Additional services that you are able to offer either yourself or through buying in specialist provision, e.g. baby ballet, horse riding, French, etc.

The key here is to really understand the needs and wants of your prospective customers, match your services to their requirements and set your prices accordingly.

Breaking even – covering your costs

Most important of all, it is essential that you understand whether you are breaking even. This means that the income from each child (less any variable costs) covers your fixed costs. This is essential to understand in order to make sure that you are not trading at a loss.

It is often the case when I speak to early years business owners that they are not aware of this important figure and are not sure how to calculate it. Only recently I was told of a setting who were convinced they were charging the right price for their services and couldn't understand why they weren't making any money. On closer examination it turned out that they were working on the basis of an 'average' break-even figure that a presenter had mentioned at a conference they had recently attended.

In order to calculate your break-even point it is essential that you have a detailed and accurate understanding of your operating costs and your expected income. So let's be a bit more specific about the information that you need to pull together in order to do this calculation for yourself.

Understanding your costs

First of all identify all your outgoings – you might find it useful to break these down using the following headings to make sure you remember everything:

- Fixed costs – those costs that stay the same regardless of your occupancy level – examples would include rent, rates, utilities, salaries and other overheads such as tax, NI and pension contributions for staff on full time contracts, insurance premiums, subscriptions, etc.

- Variable costs – these costs that are likely to fluctuate throughout the year depending on your occupancy – examples would include food and drink, craft materials, salaries and overheads for staff on flexible contracts, etc.

- Annual costs – those things that you pay for once a year – examples would include registration fees and subscriptions, etc.

- One-off costs – those things that you only pay for once, such as a new piece of equipment.

- Unexpected costs (contingency) – you may not know in advance what these will be or when they will occur but realistically every business has them. Some may be positive, for example, booking a staff member onto a course that you didn't know about at the start of the year, but most are likely to be about resolving problems, for example, a broken boiler that needs to be replaced

- Future investment – if you have plans for the future which will require a capital investment you might want to build in being able to build up that pot of money.

- Statutory reserves – as a minimum you should have enough money set aside to cover your statutory liabilities for payment of Statutory Redundancy Pay (I've covered this in more detail below).

- Profit/surplus – it's a good idea to also build into this calculation the minimum amount of profit or surplus that you want to generate.

Total up these costs for the whole year. Don't be tempted to just look at one month as this won't take account of the variability over the course of the year.

If you are just starting up or are transforming your early years business to offer different services from those that you already do, being in a position to properly estimate your total costs means putting together a detailed forecast. This will be discussed in more detail later in the chapter.

STATUTORY REDUNDANCY PAY – A REMINDER OF YOUR LEGAL OBLIGATIONS
Imagine your early years business had to close tomorrow due to an unforeseen crisis, and you immediately had to make all of your staff redundant. You should at all times keep enough money set aside, ideally in a separate account, to cover your liability to Statutory Redundancy Pay. The amount you have to pay varies each year and is calculated based on the age, length of service and salary of every member of staff employed in your business. If you employ staff who are older and have been with you for many years, this can be a very large sum of money. Here are a couple of examples:

- A staff member who is 25 years old and has worked for you for six years earning £300 per week would be entitled to £1,350.

- A senior staff member who is 55 years old and has worked for you for 20 years earning £450 per week would be entitled to £12,150.

This is a calculation you should make every year in order to make sure that you can cover this liability. If you haven't already done so, do it now as a matter of urgency. The government provides a helpful and easy to use redundancy calculator to enable you to work this out.[1]

I have often been asked by early years business owners and trustees what would happen if they simply did not have the money to pay statutory redundancy and the answer is that the government would pay staff what is owed to them from the National Insurance Fund and then take steps to recover the sums paid from the employer. Who they chase for this money depends entirely on the legal status of your early years business (see Chapter 3). If you have chosen to operate with a legal status that doesn't provide limited liability this could mean that individual owners or trustees can be pursued personally for the recovery of this money. So building up your reserves to cover your statutory liability is important and should be factored into your calculation of your outgoings.

If you are a charity, the Charity Commission recognises the significance of this problem and advises on their website: 'It is entirely legitimate for charities who have been unable to build up reserves to the desired level, to fundraise specifically for that purpose, provided that donors are made fully aware of the purpose for which the funds are required.'[2]

Next, identify all of your sources of income. Again break this down indicating how much you receive from each source. Remember to include income from Free Entitlement funding, fee income, Early Years Pupil Premium, fundraising, grant income and all other sources of income such as lettings, selling merchandise to parents, extras that you charge for, etc.

Again you should total this up for the whole year to take account of seasonal variations.

Once you have all your information together take a deep breath and complete the calculation by comparing your total outgoings, broken down to a weekly, sessional or hourly break-even figure, with your total income.

---

1   www.gov.uk/calculate-your-redundancy-pay
2   www.gov.uk/government/uploads/system/uploads/attachment_data/
     file/284723/rs5text.pdf, page 5, accessed 11 December 2016.

Unless you expect to be completely full all the way through the year, you will need to base your calculation on your predicted occupancy rate. Don't be overly optimistic with this – it's better to under-estimate your occupancy level than to over-estimate if you are using it to calculate the minimum fee that you need to charge to fee paying parents. To do the opposite would leave you in the position where you are not charging enough to cover your costs.

You might find that you need to complete the calculations more than once for different services. For example, if you are planning to open a baby room, to take on funded two-year-olds or to offer the 30 hours entitlement. The numbers work out different in each situation.

For this reason it is absolutely essential that you complete these calculations using an Excel spreadsheet or other estimating software so that you can alter figures and see the impact that your business decisions will have on your break-even.

Forecasting – the key to keeping on top of the numbers

The first step in managing the finances of your early years business on a day to day basis is accurate forecasting. This means making some sensible and well informed predictions about the money you will have coming in and the money you will need to pay out and showing this on a month by month basis. This is particularly important if you are heavily reliant on funding as a source of income, with payments being made by your local authority at irregular intervals throughout the year. An accurate forecast will enable you to:

- understand your cashflow and profitability, and how this can be impacted by changes such as changes to government funding or decisions that you make such as increasing fees to parents, changing the age profile of the children (more or fewer two-year-olds etc.), or changing your hours

- understand your profitability – this will demonstrate whether you will make a profit or surplus based on your current situation (how much your income will exceed your outgoings.) This forms what is called your Profit and Loss Statement – often called a P&L

- understand your cash flow – a cashflow forecast shows for each month what will be coming in and what will be going out – it also shows how much cash you need to put aside to cover your irregular bills and how you cope with seasonal peaks and troughs, for example, fewer children in September

- set a realistic budget for all of your activity, ensuring that you don't overspend

- plan for future investment, for example, if you have plans to expand your business

- set aside funding to cover unexpected issues (this is called contingency planning).

This sort of forecasting is essential to help you to operate your business well, but it may also be required by other bodies such as banks and other funders if you apply for any sort of loan or grant. Your financial forecasts should be incorporated into your business plan and updated regularly. Forecasting should be a regular activity to ensure financial sustainability. Many small businesses are profitable but fail because they run out of cash at certain times of the year so it's important to forecast both.

It's important to look more than one year ahead and think about how your income might change, especially in the light of the different levels of funding linked to children's ages. So ask yourself what your income looks like this year with x number of two-year-olds and what will it look like next year once those two-year-olds have become three-year-olds?

How to develop accurate financial forecasts

If you are an existing business with at least 12 months of trading behind you, then this is easy. Complete a spreadsheet showing all of your income and expenditure from last year and then look at each figure and ask yourself what will be different in the coming year. It shouldn't be guesswork, but rather should be based on an informed estimate of your income and expenditure. Some things to think about are:

- Will your income change as a result of changes to your occupancy rate or because the mix of ages of the children in your setting attracts different levels of funding, or because you will have more or fewer children for whom the Early Years Pupil Premium applies?

- Is there funding that you can apply for to boost your income? (Keep an eye out for pots of money that are announced by the government or your local authority to support various initiatives such as the Two Year Old Capital Funding or Growth Funding for Small Businesses.)

- Are there increases in your costs that you already know about such as a regular rent increase, increases to the National Living Wage and National Minimum Wage, other salary changes linked to staff completing their apprenticeship, higher legal obligations in respect of Statutory Redundancy Pay, auto-enrolment pension contributions, etc.?

- Can you predict a cost of living increase for utilities and other regular costs (not a huge amount while inflation is low but it's still a good habit to get into in case of increases in inflation in the future)?

- Do you plan to replace old equipment or redecorate your premises?

- What CPD needs have been highlighted through your staff appraisals?

- Are you hearing from colleagues in other early years businesses that certain things have suddenly become more expensive, e.g. insurance premiums?

And what do you do if you are starting up a new early years business or if you are planning to offer a service that you haven't offered before such as a baby room, or funded two-year-olds, or the 30 hours provision?

In these situations you need to do some very thorough research. Gather as much information from as many different sources as you can and then apply these (and adjust where necessary) to fit your own situation. And be prepared to do some scenario planning. This means perhaps completing your spreadsheets a number of times with each one showing a variation to cover the 'what if' situations that you might find yourself in. So a bit of thinking about the 'what ifs' is essential – what if your occupancy is lower than you predict, what if your setting up costs are higher, what if funding levels change, etc?

Tips for completing a financial forecast

- Learn to use Excel – it is essential in order to enable you to scenario plan (there are plenty of free online courses to help you if you're not confident with it).

- Gather all your information and double check with others that you haven't left anything out – you need to get a complete picture.

- Be realistic, rather than optimistic, about your predictions.

- Don't view this as a one off exercise.

Using your forecast on a day to day basis

Once you've completed your financial forecasts it's essential that these are used on a day to day basis to help you to manage your business and not just filed away in a drawer.

If you compare your actual income and expenditure with your forecast figures each month you will be able to identify any variances (positive or negative) and investigate the reasons why these have occurred. Sometimes this activity can throw up some unexpected issues: I had one client who did this and came back to me afterwards with a one word response – 'sand'. She hadn't realised and just couldn't understand how her setting was spending so much money on sand. Knowing this enabled her to put new processes in place for cleaning and reusing sand, and for reordering. Not a huge thing, of course, but this was one of lots of small changes that she made that all together meant the difference between a profit and a loss.

Reviewing your actuals regularly can also help you to spot possible trends before they become major problems. If you can spot early in the year that your phone bill seems to be regularly higher than anticipated, then you can take corrective action to resolve that issue (changing your contract or speaking to staff about using the phone less and other communication tools more). But if you wait until the end of the year it will be too late to do anything about it.

And if during the course of the year you find that something has changed and is likely to continue, then update your forecast to reflect the current situation. For example, when you hear about the next increase in the National Living Wage, adjust your forecast for the rest of the year and consider how you might need to adjust your prices to reflect this.

Balancing the books

Having completed your forecasts you will have a good idea of how your business is likely to perform over the coming year from a financial point of view. I hope this is good news and you feel happy with the outcome, but you may of course find this rather a depressing exercise and realise that you need to take some corrective action urgently to keep your business in the black.

The corrective action you can take really comes under two headings – increasing your income or reducing your costs.

Options for increasing your income
Maximising occupancy

If you are not full to capacity, then this has to be your number one priority. A marketing campaign to attract new customers to your setting is your next step. This is described in detail in Chapter 5.

Collecting all the money owed to you

Many of the early years business owners that I speak to have cashflow problems caused by parents who pay late or who run up high levels of debt and then disappear. So I'd like to cover a few thoughts about how best to manage late payment.

The right mindset

The very first thing that you must do is get yourself into the right frame of mind. All too often managers tell me that they don't take action on late payment because of how they feel about having to do this. I hear from them that the parents are like their friends, that they are nervous about upsetting them, that they want to put the child's interests first etc. etc. And this is because as a sector we employ a lot of really nice, kind people who care passionately about children – and I wouldn't for one second want to change this.

However, it's important not to allow this kindness to put you in a position where you are taken advantage of and put your business and the care it provides for all of the children (plus the jobs it provides for staff) at risk.

I'm sure you've heard it before, but it's about thinking of your early years business as any other business. You couldn't go into your local supermarket, fill your trolley with goods, get to the till and say, 'Oh, I'm sorry I've forgotten my purse today – I'll take this shopping home, and come back and pay you for it next week.' To attempt to do so would be regarded as theft!

Well, the same is true for your early years business. It is not acceptable for parents to use your services and then claim to have forgotten their purse/cheque book etc. and expect to continue to receive that service.

So your mindset needs to be that you won't allow people to treat your business like this as this jeopardises the business, the jobs of your staff and the provision for every other parent.

The right policies from day one

Your Fees Policy should set out very clearly exactly what fees will be due and when they must be paid. Make it easy for parents to pay you by introducing mechanisms such as direct debit, credit card payments, etc. You should have in place a Late Payment Policy which should be issued to parents as a part of their initial contract and a signature obtained to confirm that they have read and understood it. Your Late Payment Policy should set out clearly the steps that will be taken if a payment is late for any reason. Your policy should also cover what happens if a parent loses eligibility for 30 hours due to funding loss.

This may include charging them interest and administration fees, which you are perfectly entitled to do.[3]

---

3   www.payontime.co.uk has a useful calculator to enable you to work out easily how much you can charge, in addition to template letters and other tools.

A process to follow

It's always easier to do a difficult job if there is an established process that you just have to follow without having to think too much about what you should do next. So write a step by step process that sets out exactly what you will do as soon as a parent is late paying. Your process should include:

- checking on a weekly basis that all fees due have been paid

- having an immediate informal chat with any parent who is late paying

- template letters that just need the parent's personal details to be inserted

- a set timetable that tells you what to do, when to do it and a clear indication of whose responsibility it is to take certain actions

- clarity about when things need to be escalated to senior management, owners or your committee, or to begin the formal process of debt collection.

Follow your process

As with any process, it only works if you follow it. So follow the process to the letter regardless of the situation. As soon as you start making exceptions because you feel sorry for a parent or because you know them well and feel that you can trust them, you're on a very slippery slope. In some cases where you have a personal relationship with the parent, consider whether you are the best person to deal with the outstanding payment. I have in the past in my business used my PA to do this. And she was extremely good at it. I can recall meeting up with the client who had been late paying an invoice and being told that my accounts manager was a bit scary on the phone! I was able to distance myself from any bad feeling about the situation and take the opportunity to discuss how to prevent financial difficulties arising again in the future (to guarantee no more calls from my scary accounts manager – my PA).

Be prepared to escalate it

There may be times when your internal process fails to resolve the situation. In these cases you need to be prepared to follow your process through and escalate it. This might mean commissioning a solicitor to write a letter for you (any costs incurred become a part of the debt owed to you by the parent) or to take them to the small claims court. Often these actions (or even the threat of them) can resolve the problem. I had one situation a couple of years ago where I phoned a client and informed them that I had just completed the online form for the court application and just wanted to confirm that I had the correct postcode before pressing the submit button. All of a sudden they found a way to pay me and the money appeared in my bank account within the hour. If handling this yourself feels daunting then consider using a professional debt collection service. They will charge you a fee, but again this is added to the amount of the debt owed to you, ensuring that you and your business are not out of pocket.

Signing up to accept Tax-Free Childcare payments

Tax-Free Childcare is a new government scheme being launched in 2017 to help working parents with the cost of childcare (replacing the old system of Childcare Vouchers, which is being phased out in 2018). Under the new scheme parents open an online account with National Savings and Investments (NS&I), which they can use to pay for childcare from a registered provider.

For every £8 a parent pays in, the government will pay in an extra £2. Parents can receive up to £2,000 per child, per year, towards their childcare costs (or £4,000 for children with disabilities).

The scheme will be available for children up to the age of 12, or 17 for children with disabilities.

To qualify, parents will have to be in work, and each earning at least the equivalent of 16 hours a week (at National Living Wage) and not more than £100,000 per year, and not be receiving support through Tax Credits or Universal Credit.

Only childcare providers registered with Ofsted can receive Tax-Free Childcare payments, and you must register your setting with the scheme in order to receive payments in this way. Once you sign up, you'll appear on the government's online list, which lets parents search for childcare providers signed up for Tax-Free Childcare. Parents will be able to send you payments by BACS directly from their Tax-Free Childcare account to your bank account.[4] The same online registration system is being used to deliver 30 hours funded provision.

The previous system of employer supported childcare continues to be available for current members if they wish to remain in it, or they can switch to the new scheme.

Applying for funding

Many small businesses, not just those in the early years and childcare sector tell me that, since the 2008 recession, there is no longer any external funding which they can access. Although it is probably true to say that a lot of funding was withdrawn for a while, it is also the case that funding streams have come back online and new sources of funding have been launched.

But there are differences. The current funding streams:

- require a bit of detective work to locate them (in days gone by the Business Link service tended to be a one stop shop for accessing a range of services including advice on funding – this is no longer available to us)

- often provide loans at competitive rates rather than grants (in other words there is an expectation that they will result in a business being more successful and being able to repay the funding provided)

- often require matched funding (in other words they expect you to raise an equivalent sum of money – or more – from other sources)

- are more competitively fought over (this means that you need to be able to write a very convincing business case in order to be successful in applying for funding).

In this table I have outlined some of the sources of funding that early years providers might typically access with a few examples of each (contact details correct at time of going to print).

---

4   Further information about the Tax-Free Childcare Scheme can be found at www. gov.uk/government/news/tax-free-childcare-top-things-childcare-providers-should-know.

Funding source	Examples include:	Suitable for:
Trusts and grants	www.bbc.co.uk/programmes/b008dk4b/features/grants (Children in Need) www.comicrelief.com www.mindthegap.org.uk http://esmeefairbairn.org.uk www.footballfoundation.org.uk/funding-schemes http://educationendowmentfoundation.org.uk/apply-for-funding www.trusthousecharitablefoundation.org.uk www.communitybuildersfund.org.uk www.theguardian.com/society/series/charity-awards-2016	Charities or social enterprises – but very competitive often with specific application deadlines
Grant-finding services	www.grants4growth.org.uk www.open4funding.info www.j4bgrants.co.uk www.fundingcentral.org.uk www.familylearningnetwork.com www.governmentfunding.org.uk	Charities or social enterprises – some are free to register with, others charge a fee
Government grants	www.childcarebusinessgrants.dcms.gov.uk	Small start-up grants for all types of early years providers
Community Foundations	http://ukcommunityfoundations.org	Charities or social enterprises – Community Foundations manage lots of small pots of funding – search for your local community to find what's available in your area

Business support organisations	www.princes-trust.org.uk/help-for-young-people/support-starting-business www.bizbritain.com www.nationalenterprisenetwork.org/business-directory www.gov.uk/government/publications/local-enterprise-partnerships-map www.bitc.org.uk/all_programmes	Any small businesses – often provide mentoring support in addition to low cost finance
National Lottery	www.biglotteryfund.org.uk/prog_reaching_communities (£10,000–£500,000) www.awardsforall.org.uk (£300–£10,000)	Charities or social enterprises – Awards for All is ideal for settings wanting to apply for smaller sums of money
Crowdfunding	www.buzzbnk.org www.fundingcircle.com www.crowdfunder.co.uk	Suitable for all types of settings – can be used as a way of attracting investors who expect a commercial return (also called Peer-to-Peer Lending), but also used purely to fundraise
Fundraising	www.localgiving.com www.institute-of-fundraising.org.uk	Charities or social enterprises
Corporate giving/CSR	www.bitc.org.uk www.payrollgivingcentre.com www.lloydsbankfoundation.org.uk www.focusedlearning.co.uk/portfoli/helping.htm www.sjpfoundation.co.uk www.johnlewispartnership.co.uk/csr/our-community/charitable-foundations-and-trust.html www.chelmsfordstar.coop/community/community-home www.tescoplc.com/index.asp?pageid=120 www.diy.com/diy/jsp/corporate/content/environment_ethics/ethics/community/index.jsp	Charities or social enterprises – many commercial organisations have a CSR Policy and/or a Community Engagement Manager

Funding source	Examples include:	Suitable for:
Philanthropists /Business Angels	www.philanthropyuk.org/grant-seekers www.ukbusinessangelsassociation.org.uk	Suitable for all types of settings – can be used as a way of attracting investors who expect a commercial return (also referred to as Venture Capitalists), but also used purely to fundraise
Online retail schemes	www.simplyfundraising.co.uk www.thegivingmachine.co.uk	Charities or social enterprises – very simple way to enable your supporters to generate donations while they shop online
Loans	www.charitybank.org www.triodos.co.uk www.unity.co.uk www.foundationeast.org www.burnleysavingsandloans.co.uk (Bank of Dave) www.fundingcircle.com (Peer to peer lending) www.cdfa.org.uk/funding-and-development/ (Community Development Finance Association) www.princes-trust.org.uk (low interest start up loans if under 30) www.futurebuilders-england.org.uk/are-you-eligible responsiblefinance.org.uk	Suitable for all types of settings who want to borrow and who have found the High Street banks unsupportive – some focus on charities, others focus on a particular location
Pro-bono professional services	www.prohelp.org.uk www.lawsociety.org.uk/lfyb www.icaew.com	Charities or social enterprises – sources of pro-bono (free) professional services rather than a source of funding if you have a project that needs professional support
Local Government grants	Ask your local counsellors/local authority website/planning department about locality grants/s106 funding/CIL (Community Infrastructure Levy)	Suitable for all types of settings that want to set up or expand provision in areas highlighted by the local authority as being in need of additional childcare places

Increasing your prices process

One of the most obvious ways of increasing your income is of course to increase your fees. Again this is something that over the years I have found many early years business owners to be reluctant to do. Reasons usually revolve around the fear that 'we'd lose all our parents', which anyone who has increased their fees will tell you simply doesn't happen.

So here are a few thoughts about building price increases into your financial planning.

The right mindset

Yes, this is the first place to start again. Acknowledging that you are running a business (even if it is a business run on a charitable basis) is the first thing to think about. This means that you have obligations to shareholders (maybe yourself), to current and future beneficiaries (i.e. parents and children) if you running a charity, to your staff etc. And your key obligation is to ensure that the business is sustainable. Making sure that the amount you charge is sufficient to cover your costs and to generate a profit or surplus is the first requirement of business sustainability.

It's also important to remind yourself that increasing costs, even in these times of record low inflation, are a fact of life. Think about your costs for a moment – which of those have increased over the past 12 months (wages, insurance premiums, utilities, etc.) and which are likely to increase over the coming 12 months? And in the 12 months after that?

The right policies from day one

Acknowledge in your fees policy that covering your costs in order to operate the business sustainably is the key factor that determines your fees. Making this clear to parents from day one means that you don't need to constantly provide a justification for any future increases in fees. Make sure that you write price reviews into your contract with parents. Once or twice a year is fine. And note that I have used the phrase 'price reviews' and not 'price increases'. There is nothing to stop you reviewing your prices and deciding that no increase is required. How nice to be able to send a letter to parents saying: 'We have reviewed our prices in line with our policy and on this occasion have decided that no increase is required to enable us to continue to operate sustainably'. When you next review your prices and decide that an increase is due, you can remind them by saying: 'You'll remember that when we last reviewed our prices we were able to keep them the same. So you'll not be surprised that on this occasion we do need to make a small increase to make sure that we continue to cover our costs'.

A process to follow

Your process with regards to fee increases should begin with a thorough analysis of your financial forecast. If you have done the prior work of pulling together a financial forecast and calculating your break-even price then this should be quite straightforward. Knowing your reason for any price increase will again help you to present it appropriately to parents.

Giving sufficient advance notice in writing is important. Families need to be able to budget for increases in fees. And think about the timing. If the majority of your parents work in jobs where their pay is reviewed annually, with any increases applied in April, then applying your fee increase in April makes it feel less of a burden.

Most early years businesses that I work with give about half a term's notice of fee increases, so about six weeks.

Communicate assertively

When you tell parents about a fee increase do it in an assertive and business-like manner. You may wish to explain why it is necessary (i.e., to cover your increased costs) and perhaps to give some examples of increased costs that parents will be able to relate to from their own personal experiences, for example minimum wage increase, insurance premiums, gas bills etc. But remember that an explanation is not the same as an apology. Does your electricity company apologise for increasing their prices? Well, neither should you.

Another way of increasing your fees is to simply make sure that you are charging parents for all of the additional elements of the service that you are providing them. It's quite easy in business to keep adding to your service offer in an effort to offer continuous improvement and innovation, and to find that you are adding costs into your service which you are then not recouping from customers. This is a slippery slope towards operating at a loss.

So, every time you add something new, cost it out and think about how you should cover that cost as a part of your fees.

This is of course more challenging where you are providing care for children who are taking funded hours only. Great care should be taken to ensure you fully understand what you are permitted to charge for in respect of those children so as not to fall foul of the 'no top-up fees' rules.

Options for reducing your outgoings

Increasing costs are unfortunately a part of life and a part of the life of any business. Even during periods of low inflation, some costs seem to keep rising. Some of the most significant cost increases noticed by early years businesses during recent years have been: increases to the National Minimum Wage and the introduction of the National Living Wage, business rates, premises rents (especially for those who have traditionally rented premises from local authorities on 'peppercorn rents'), compliance costs, and training costs under the government's new Apprenticeships scheme.

Tips for reducing your costs

The key here is to reduce costs without reducing quality of provision.

- Once you have a detailed cash flow forecast in place it becomes much easier to review your actual expenditure on a month by month basis and identify areas where your costs are higher than they should be.

- Make a point of benchmarking with other providers that you meet to see whether you should look at cutting your costs in certain areas.

- Get your staff involved in thinking about ways that costs can be managed. Many organisations find that offering staff members a small incentive to come up with ideas can be very motivational and a good way to make them feel involved in important decisions about the provision. Also consider giving room leaders a budget for toys, consumables, etc. as this gives them a sense of ownership and may result in cost savings.

- Get into the habit of always shopping around for a better deal rather than simply allowing contracts for services to renew automatically. These days it is so much easier to do with all the comparison sites that exist on the internet. Many suppliers will automatically price match if you can demonstrate that you have been quoted a better price elsewhere. So, be prepared by getting a revised price, even if you would prefer to stay with your existing supplier, and then use that revised price to negotiate a better deal with them. And, at the end of the day, be prepared to move if they are unable to give you a better deal.

- Following on from that, develop keen negotiation skills and be prepared to haggle – remember 'if you don't ask, you don't get'.

Flexible staffing

For early years and childcare businesses, staff salaries and benefits make up by far the largest proportion of our outgoings. So, looking for ways to manage this large element of our expenditure is essential.

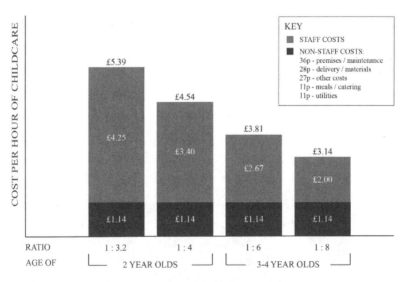

Representative unit costs (voluntary group-based providers)

Adapted from the Department for Education (2015)
Review of Childcare Costs: The Analytical Report

Sam Gyimah MP, when he held a childcare brief for the government, commented that 'potentially big savings are available using more variable staffing models to recognise peaks and troughs in occupancy'.[5] So the first thing to consider is your staff ratios.

Many early years businesses are prepared to work with a higher ratio of staff than is legally required because this is a significant selling point that many parents are attracted to, and can also result in higher staff morale. However, this comes at a cost. If you are in a position to pass those higher costs on to your parents through higher fees, then that's fine, but if you are not, then you really do need to consider your staff ratios. This might mean asking staff to work more flexibly within your business, moving between different rooms according to occupancy levels. In some settings it works best to have core staff supplemented by 'floating' team members who can be located in whichever room requires the extra body. One of my clients calls these staff members 'Butterflies'. And if you do the sums, you may well find that having one or two staff members above the legal minimum can actually save you money; there are always unplanned staff absences for training and sickness that need to be covered and paying for agency over is horrendously expensive.

Introducing flexible contracts of employment can also be a big help in managing the fluctuating occupancy levels which many settings experience linked to schools' start dates. Many early years businesses that operate on a term time only basis already use term time only contracts very successfully, but there are other forms of flexible contracts which you might also consider. These include:

- *Term time working*: where employees are on a permanent contract but can take paid or unpaid leave during school holidays only – the reverse holiday time working may also apply.

- *Job-sharing*: where two people share the responsibility for a job between them – this requires careful consideration in our context because of the need to ensure continuity of care for childcare.

---

5   www.gov.uk/government/uploads/system/uploads/attachment_data/file/479662/151124_Exec_Summary_Analytical_review_FINAL_VERSION.pdf, page 9, accessed 12 December 2016.

- *Flexitime*: where employees can choose, within certain set limits, when to begin and end work. Core hours might be set by the employer to cover times when the setting is full with the flexibility being applied during quieter periods.

- *Compressed hours*: where working hours are reallocated into fewer, longer days during the week, for example, to accommodate longer opening times and the 30 hours extended entitlement.

- *Annualised hours*: where the total number of hours to be worked over the year is fixed in advance but there is variation over the year in the length of the working day and week in order to manage seasonal variations in occupancy; pay is equalised over the whole year so the employee doesn't experience huge variations in their income.

- *Working from home*: where employees regularly spend time working from home; can be useful for allowing team leaders and managers to complete required paperwork and planning activity if space is an issue within the setting but may adversely affect ratios.

- *Zero hours contracts*: where an employee has no guarantee of a minimum number of working hours, but can be called upon as and when required, and paid just for the hours they work. Building up your own bank of staff on zero hours contracts can be a good alternative to calling on temporary or agency staff when cover is required.

And remember of course that your staff are legally entitled to request flexible working arrangements. You should have a policy in place to deal with this, examples of which can be found on the ACAS website.

There is nothing to stop you from introducing new flexible contracts for new staff joining your setting in the future, but changing the contracts of existing staff can be more problematic. Contracts cannot be changed legally without proper consultation. The guidance provided on the ACAS website takes you through the process that you would need to use if you decided that you wanted to introduce more flexible contracts for existing staff.

Other financial management considerations

Aside from managing your income and expenditure, there are a few other financial management considerations to take into account.

Banking

The banking environment is constantly changing, with increasing regulation and competition making it imperative for banks to provide a better deal for customers. But all too often, small business customers can end up being tied into a deal that really doesn't suit their needs and costs them a fortune.

Before committing to a particular banking arrangement, think carefully about the current and future needs of your business. This checklist will help you to think through the various factors involved in choosing a suitable bank for your early years business.

- Know what you need/want from your banking arrangements and make a list – examples might include:

  » a face to face manager to advise you on business matters

  » credit card

  » local banking/ATMs

  » online banking.

- Decide how and when you prefer to deal with your bank (online, telephone, in branch, at your local Post Office, outside of normal banking hours, etc.).

- If you get a good deal as a new customer, are you prepared for the upheaval of moving your account once that introductory deal comes to an end? If you are, diarise to review it when the deal ends. If not, don't be tempted in by introductory offers, go for the best longer term deal instead.

- Fees and charges will vary depending on the sort of transactions will you be making, so think about your current and future use of cash, direct debits, credit card payments, etc.

- Does the bank you are considering have a good reputation for customer service?

- If you anticipate that at some point in the future you might wish to borrow from your bank, either for a specific project such as new premises, or to assist with short term cash flow needs, it is essential that you speak to a bank manager early rather than wait until you are desperate. Ask them to outline for you their lending criteria, and to help you to understand how best to demonstrate to the bank that your business is a good risk.

Book-keeping and accounting

One of the decisions you need to make about managing your finances, is the extent to which you will manage things in house versus the extent to which you will outsource activities to external professionals. There is no right answer to this question but you do need to weigh up factors such as:

- Do you have the skills and knowledge to manage your finances competently?

- How much time you are prepared to commit to managing your finances on a day to day basis? Often a qualified professional can do things in a fraction of the time that it takes you to do them yourself.

- How complex are your financial arrangements?

- Do you have access to suitable software that can make it easy to manage your finances and can automate certain processes?

Whatever you decide, here are a few good housekeeping tips that are relevant in all situations:

Separate business and personal money

Don't mix personal and business finances. In some cases, such as childminders, or early years businesses where an owner is running a very small setting on a sole trader basis, it can be tempting to view the business and the individual as one and the same, moving money between the two without clear dividing lines.

As you can imagine the taxman gets very uncomfortable with this sort of arrangement, especially if cash is involved. So it is important to have a separate bank account for your business. If you are a sole trader, this need not be a 'business account' (which banks will charge you more to run) but can simply be a separate current account in your own name that you only use for business purposes.

Treat the business as a separate entity from which you only take income in the form of wages (known as 'drawings' for sole traders), dividends (in the case of limited companies), and in claiming back business expenses against receipts.

Make sure all cash payments received from parents go through the bank. It is tempting if fees are received in cash to simply pocket that money and use it to pay for items for your business such as shopping for food, etc. Again, the taxman gets very uncomfortable with this sort of arrangement as the cash effectively becomes invisible. So always make sure that cash payments are banked and then withdrawn in order to show a proper audit trail of where the money has gone so it can be properly accounted for.

In a sole trader situation the model looks like this:

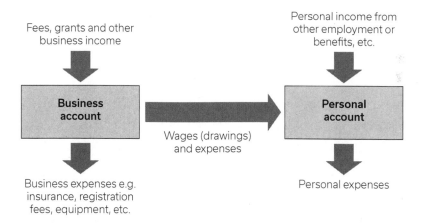

Fees, grants and other business income

Personal income from other employment or benefits, etc.

Business account

Wages (drawings) and expenses

Personal account

Business expenses e.g. insurance, registration fees, equipment, etc.

Personal expenses

Systems to help you manage your money

Spend time setting up a system which you know you can stick to. It doesn't have to be a complicated or expensive system; a simple Excel spreadsheet may be all that you require in the early stages of your business (in fact, I still use the same Excel spreadsheets today that

I put in place when I started my business 15 years ago, with a few adaptations along the way).

There are many suppliers of nursery management software which you may find helpful in running larger, more complex early years businesses. Many of these enable you to manage invoicing, rotas and ratios, accounts etc. all in the same place. A number of these are listed on the Day Nurseries website and offer a free trial or free demo.

It's essential to keep on top of your financial administration on a day to day basis. Allocate a regular time every week/month to deal with financial administration. Don't let it pile up or things are likely to get overlooked and forgotten about, and mistakes are likely to be made.

File your records logically and in order. Again, do this as you go along rather than saving your filing for a day when you have time to do it. That day never seems to come.

And as mentioned previously in this chapter, have systems in place for dealing with problems such as late paying customers.

Financial security matters

Consider who should be involved in financial administration within your early years business; the fewer people involved, the fewer errors are likely to creep in. But do make sure that you have two signatories for all cheques.

Password-protect or encrypt financial records held electronically, and only share the password with a few people (do not leave your password on a post-it note on the wall in the office, as I have often seen, or stuck on the bottom of your laptop).

Increasingly we undertake many of our financial transactions online, which is great as it means we can sort out our banking matters on a Sunday afternoon but does create issues around keeping safe online. Here are a few things that you can do to improve online security:

- Use strong passwords for all online/telephone banking transactions – consider using a random password generator to ensure your passwords are as strong as possible.

- Change your passwords from time to time.

- Set up alerts to inform you of any unusual activity on your accounts.

- Protect your financial information from internet fraud scams such as phishing, hackers and viruses by using good internet security software and making sure that it updates automatically.

Keep a regular electronic back-up of all your electronic data. Ideally this should be an automated process so that you don't have to remember to do it yourself. Many inexpensive back-up systems run invisibly in the background so that you're not interrupted in any way (I have mine set to back-up every hour). If you are creating a physical back-up onto an external hard drive, this should be kept off-site in case of a fire at your premises. Or consider a cloud-based back-up using a reliable UK-based provider.

Set up a systematic way of regularly checking/auditing your finances, especially in relation to expenses and petty cash. This is important as a fraud avoidance measure. Businesses who fail to do this and subsequently suffer fraudulent activity are likely to find that their insurance provider views them as negligent and refuses to pay out. Reconcile your actual expenditure against your forecast and look out for anything that is unexpected or unusual.

Keep your financial records, including any supporting information and documents filed safely in case they are required by HMRC as part of an investigation. They expect you to retain the current year's paperwork plus the previous six years. Store records that can't be scanned and copied, for example, chequebook stubs and paying-in books, in a fireproof box. Think about where these records are stored. One of my clients stored their last six years accounts in their loft and felt confident when HMRC arrived on their doorstep to conduct an investigation. Imagine how they felt when they retrieved their boxes of records and found that they had been inhabited by squirrels and completely destroyed. Remember in this situation, HMRC will estimate the tax owed and are unlikely to give you the benefit of the doubt. It cost this particular setting in excess of £30,000.

Also think carefully about how you dispose of financial paperwork once you no longer need it. Even if it is several years old make sure that you shred it all before recycling it.

Chapter 5

FINDING AND KEEPING CUSTOMERS

Many of the early years businesses that I encounter do not have a marketing plan. Some do a bit of marketing, perhaps on rather an ad-hoc basis; others tend to rely purely on word of mouth. But at a time of increasing competition, with new players such as schools and academies coming into the market, a good marketing plan becomes a more important component within your Early Years Business Dashboard.

Effective marketing provides information about your services in a way that makes it easier for parents to make the decision to use you. This might be because:

- they have more information about your service

- they understand how it meets their needs

- they associate your service with something that is important to them

- they understand how your service can be accessed.

Word of mouth is, of course, a great form of marketing – it's highly credible and it's free – but sometimes this isn't enough, particularly if you are launching a new service, or transforming the way you operate, or if you need to repair a damaged reputation, for example, following a poor Ofsted report or a change of ownership.

So, this chapter looks at how to produce a marketing plan that is designed to attract new customers cost effectively, and that also makes use of a range of methods in order to get your message across to potential customers.

I will explore how to build techniques into your plan such as use of testimonials, reviews, special offers and discounts and also how to make your marketing appealing and attractive to prospective customers. I will also consider the importance of retaining existing customers.

The significance of brand and reputation

Having a clear and recognisable brand for your early years business can make it much easier for parents to notice you in a crowded and competitive marketplace. Your business brand can be represented by things such as a logo (e.g., Apple), a strapline (e.g., Tesco: Every Little Helps), a sound (e.g., Intel) or by a personality (e.g., Richard Branson: Virgin). If your brand is a significant differentiator for your business it can be protected legally through the registering of a trademark to prevent anyone else from using it. This is quite expensive but might be important to your business depending on your plans for future expansion.

Reputation can be defined as what people think about you: your image in the childcare marketplace. Developing a positive reputation is essential and will make it easier to attract new customers. Reputation can take a long time to build but only seconds to destroy; an example of this being Gerald Ratner whose light-hearted description of the products sold in his high street jewelry shops as 'total crap' during an after-dinner speech in 1991 wiped £500 million off the value of his business literally overnight.

Undertaking research to find out what parents and other people in the early years sector think about your business can be a valuable exercise.

Developing a socially responsible reputation

Being recognised as a socially responsible business may be something that matters to you and to the parents you wish to attract.

Small businesses wishing to enhance this aspect of their reputation can do so in many ways and the Organisation for Responsible Businesses (ORB) seeks to advise and support those businesses in achieving this. Their ethos is 'People Planet Profit' and they suggest businesses that want to be considered responsible should think about how they demonstrate responsible behaviour in the following areas:

Workplace

A trained, engaged and motivated workforce will result in less absenteeism, reduced staff turnover and more productivity. Your workforce is your business's greatest asset and should be treated as such.

Environment

Legislation continues to increase and early years businesses are required to adhere to specific rules and regulations which can seem to increase costs. But businesses can make huge savings on costs such as paper, waste disposal, water, heating and transport by choosing environmentally-friendly options.

Community

Considering the needs of your local community can boost your reputation and have a considerable positive impact on your business. Early years businesses are well placed to do this, providing, as they do, services that are at the heart of their local community. Sourcing supplies and recruiting locally will also help support the local economy. Engagement in community activities can do much to enhance your reputation – and can be fun!

The marketplace

How well do you look after your suppliers, partners and customers? Can you make any improvements to the way that you work with them? Do you know anything about the goods that you purchase for use in your early years business; could they, for example, have been made by child labour or from materials that are not from a sustainable source?

Values and transparency

Do you operate in an open, honest and transparent way with your staff, with parents, with suppliers, and with other stakeholders such as partners or the local authority? Be clear about your personal ethics and build them into your business and communicate this with everyone that comes into contact with your business.

The Responsible Business Standard, which the ORBL operates, is an externally audited standard which small businesses that wish to enhance their reputation as responsible businesses can apply for. It audits practice across each of these five areas.

Socially responsible marketing

If you decide that it's important for your business to be regarded as socially responsible then socially responsible marketing that is aligned with this ambition is also essential. I'm going to make the assumption that this is the case and discuss it in more detail (but feel free to skip this section if it's not something that matters to you).

Socially responsible marketing can be described as marketing that considers and respects the needs of potential customers and of society as a whole, as well as the need of your business to generate new customers and sell services.

It might incorporate aspects of your business's ethical code such as environmental considerations, for example, by ensuring that all your brochures and information packs are printed on recycled paper, or sent to parents digitally, or perhaps a religious ethos for settings that are attached to a church or other faith institution.

It is essential, therefore, that you have an understanding of your core values and that these are clearly expressed throughout your marketing communications. Your values should also be represented in every other aspect of your business. So, for example, if you claim to provide services that enhance people's living standards but employ staff on salaries below the National Living Wage, or if you claim to consider the environment in your business activity but drive a 'gas guzzler' – this might be seen as incoherent and it would dilute and undermine your message about being a socially responsible business.

So basing your reputation around your core values isn't just about what you say in your marketing communications, it's about walking the talk – demonstrating those values in every aspect of your day to day behaviour.

You should be careful when publicising your core values as a part of your branding as this creates an expectation in the minds of customers and others, and may result in your early years business being criticised if it fails to live up to those values. So be very clear that those values that you claim to espouse are absolutely at the heart of your business.

Socially responsible marketing may be very important to your various stakeholders, for example, if you are operating as a charity and hope to raise funds through donations or sponsorship. Alternatively for a commercial business, it may not be a consideration for your customers at all.

So it is important to consult with a range of stakeholders in developing socially responsible marketing. Customers and sponsors should be asked what matters to them and which causes they support so that you know what you should include in your business and marketing plans. Causes that matter to parents might include things like Fairtrade or Buy Local. Any staff or volunteers who will be involved in fundraising activity should then be briefed on your values and your social responsibility policies so that they understand how they are expected to behave when representing the setting to potential donors. A poor example of this recently has been the use by some charities of aggressive fundraising behaviour. This has damaged the reputation of the charities concerned.

So, if you decide that socially responsible marketing is the right thing for you to do you need to make sure that any marketing that you do:

- is honest

- doesn't mislead people in any way

- doesn't seek to exploit vulnerable people (including children)

- seeks to avoid having a negative impact on the environment, the community, etc.

- adheres to the standards of ethics that you embrace e.g., Fairtrade, organic, buy local, low carbon

- meets regulatory standards and those promoted by bodies such as the Advertising Standards Authority.

Why produce a marketing plan?

A well thought through marketing plan will make sure that you spend your time and money on the right sort of marketing activities. It will also put you in a position where you can properly evaluate what works and what doesn't so that you can focus future activity on the right kinds of things. It is easy to spend a fortune on marketing, so I would always encourage you to concentrate on cost effective marketing methods that will attract new customers and increase your occupancy for minimum outlay.

Key elements of a marketing plan

A good marketing plan should consider the following questions about your business:

What is your business seeking to achieve?

Your marketing plan should be based on your business objectives as set out in your Early Years Business Dashboard. So, for example, are you seeking to expand your business, launch new services, transform your business, or just attract a few more customers? Doing this thinking first will make sure that you don't waste money, time and effort on inappropriate marketing activity.

Targeting

Let's imagine that a new housing estate with 100 new houses has been built close to your setting and you've decided to market your services to people moving into those homes. So you go and get 100 fliers printed and put them through the doors of the 100 houses on the estate.

A percentage of those houses may be currently unoccupied. Others may be lived in by people who simply gather your leaflet up with all the other junk mail and put it in the bin, people with no children, parents with older children, parents who have already sorted out their childcare arrangements, parents who might be interested and put your leaflet somewhere safe to look at another day (then forget about it). You get the picture. So out of your 100 leaflets how many do you think will result in an enquiry?

Statistically this sort of 'mass marketing' is shown to elicit a less than 1 per cent response rate. So that means 99 of your lovely (expensive) leaflets go to waste!

Targeted marketing, on the other hand, involves taking some time in advance to identify those people who are most likely to be interested in using your service and specifically targeting your marketing towards them. This means investing more in what we call market research and less in the actual marketing activities themselves. Statistically, a well targeted marketing campaign might elicit up to a 40 per cent response rate.

In the case of my example, this might mean identifying those houses where there are parents with young children living and going to speak to them. Maybe engaging them in conversation. Maybe asking them to pass your leaflet onto other parents they know who are in a similar situation to them. If you are a pre-school offering sessional care between 09.00 and 15.00 then you are probably going to be looking for parents who are at home with their children, who work part time, or who have other childcare available to them. If, on the other hand, you are a nursery offering full day care from 08.00 to 19.00, then working families who perhaps have to commute might be your target customers. Targeting people also avoids the risk of annoying other local people by sending them irrelevant spam or junk mail.

Tailoring content to appeal to different target audiences will also make any marketing that you do more effective. This activity is often referred to as market segmentation. Defining market segments will enable you to target your services towards potential customers who have a need to buy them. It also enables you to design your marketing in such a way that it is likely to appeal to those customers.

Customers can be segmented in various ways. For your early years business it might be useful to segment customers using the following criteria:

- *funding source*: free entitlement funding only, parent fees

- *working pattern*: full time employees, part time but eligible for 30 hours free entitlement, working fewer hours, not working, commuters

- *location*: walking distance, live in surrounding villages, work nearby, passing through close to your setting.

Think about how you might be able to offer your services more flexibly in order to appeal to different market segments. This is because customers in different market segments have different needs and different buying capacity. So, consider if the different segments you have identified are likely to be most in need of full day, sessional or after school care, holiday clubs, flexible hours, 30 hours, etc.

There are many different ways that marketing professionals gather this sort of data about potential customers. This might include:

• Inviting visitors to your website to sign up for a newsletter or to register their email address in order to download a brochure or a freebie, e.g. a report about a topic of interest. There are a number of tools that can be used to make it easier for a business to capture digital data. Auto complete forms on websites which make use of Cookies are an example of this. Use of Cookies enhances the experience for a visitor to your website by remembering which pages they visited previously and showing them what you believe to be relevant information which will be of interest to them. Cookies also mean that repeat visitors don't have to keep putting their information into your forms again. Providing a warning on your website that your site uses Cookies is required, as is allowing people to opt out of that and to have any information captured about them deleted. Tools such as Google Analytics can be used to capture and report on data about the behaviour of visitors to your website. There are similar tools allowing you to report on engagements through social media platforms.

• Buying in lists – this is time efficient, but expensive and may not be reliable; lists need to be validated (consider buying a sample and testing it for accuracy first). Another danger of purchasing lists is that people haven't given their permission for their details to be sold/passed on. The best way to build a database of contacts is therefore to collect details yourself as it is fair to assume that if someone gives you their details they are happy for you to market to them. Even in this situation, it's still best practice to ask for their permission. You should also ensure that you always give people an option to opt-out of any further contact and to have their details removed from your records. Tools like Mail Chimp and Constant Contact enable you to do this automatically.

• Attending face to face networking events, local exhibitions, and community events and asking people who visit your stand to enter a prize draw in exchange for giving their email address.

(Again ensure they tick to allow you to contact them for marketing purposes.)

- Engaging with parents via social media and other online sources; this is easy to do and costs nothing but is time consuming and you may not find the information you need.

- Employing a market research agency, which is time efficient but very expensive.

- Asking existing customers and staff; this is easy to do and a really positive activity as it builds the relationship based on a trusted referral, but it can be time consuming and you need to develop a consistent way of capturing and analysing this information.

Finding out about prospective customers

It is important to decide what data you need before you begin to conduct any market research. Some examples of the type of information you might be interested in are given below.

- What kind of childcare do they want, e.g. full day, 30 hours, pre-school, after school club, etc.?

- How far are they prepared to travel?

- How much are they prepared to pay?

- What do they think about what's currently available?

- What do they think/know about your setting?

- Do they currently use any other providers of childcare and are they likely to continue to do so in the future?

I often ask early years businesses if they conduct any market research and they say that they do, but when asked for more detail they acknowledge that they only research the needs of their existing customers.

This might be helpful if what you are looking for is more of the same types of customers, but if you are considering making a change to your business, such as considering if you should open longer to provide services to working parents, then the parents you need to research are those that you don't currently have a relationship with, those that currently don't regard your setting as meeting their needs. So how can you make contact with those parents and find out what they need/want?

Tips on using surveys

Surveys can be a very valuable market research tool, so here are a few tips about how best to design and use a survey.

- Be clear about what you want to find out and why (so don't ask questions just for the sake of it).

- Keep it short.

- Use simple language and test it first.

- Make it easy for people to complete:

  » Use tick boxes, multiple choice, graded answers, etc.

  » Approach people face to face at times when they are hanging around, e.g., when they are waiting in the playground to collect older children from school, provide a pen, complete it for them, provide an online survey, e.g. using SurveyMonkey.

  » Provide a reply paid envelope so they can easily return a paper survey.

- Incentivise it (what could you offer to make it worth their while to complete, e.g., appeal to their philanthropy by making a donation to charity for every survey completed, or offer a free session).

- Offer to share the results with them – people are often interested to know how they compare with others.

- Demonstrate that you have acted on the results (many of the schools I work with put a section on their website following parental surveys saying: 'You said…we've done…')

- Ask if you can capture their contact details, but allow them to complete it anonymously if they prefer.

Social media can be used to find out more about both customers and competitors in the following ways:

- Observe what parents say about your competitors by viewing comments made on their Facebook page or LinkedIn profile.

- Follow competitors, customers and prospective customers on Twitter to see what they are talking about/what's important to them (this can be done discreetly by creating Private Lists).

- Invite people to participate in an online poll or survey about your services by sending it out via social media (e.g., we're thinking about extending our opening hours – which would you prefer 07.30–18.00 or 08.00–18.30?).

- Offer your Twitter followers or Facebook fans a taster session, discount or special offer on a new service in exchange for giving you feedback about it to support its development.

Social media is a useful medium for conducting market research because it's free and easy to use, and because people tend to openly share a lot of information about themselves on social media, meaning that you can build an in-depth understanding of them. It enables you to:

- see what parents say about your competitors by viewing Endorsements or Recommendations on their LinkedIn profile (in addition to reading reviews on sites such as Rate My Nursery or Good Care Guide). Research can even be conducted covertly/anonymously for example by creating a Private List in Twitter

- invite parents to participate in an online poll or survey about your services by sending it out via social media

- follow competitors on Twitter to see what they are talking about or even conduct competitor research covertly/anonymously by creating a Private List in Twitter

- keep up to date with news and changes affecting your setting and your customers quickly and easily.

Knowing how you compare

Market research may also involve doing some research about your competitors so that you know how you compare. This can help you to design your services and position your early years business so as to be more attractive to parents. So typically you might want to find out:

- How many providers are there in your area?

- Is there an over supply of places or a shortage?

- How many of them offer what your target customers want?

- Are there new settings opening?

- What do your competitors offer?

- How much do they charge?

- What do parents think of them?

Some tried and tested methods of conducting competitor research include:

Website review – it shocks me sometimes how much information settings put onto their websites; you can find out an awful lot about them without having to leave your armchair. However, be aware that the information on their website might be out of date and might not be accurate (remember also that this is their marketing so only tells you what they want to say). Independent sources[1] might give you a more independent view as will the Ofsted website where you'll find their Ofsted reports.[2]

Ask other people what they think – staff who have worked for your competitors or been interviewed by them, prospective customers who come for a look around have probably also been to visit your competitors.

Ask them directly – there is no harm in approaching your competitors directly in the spirit of sharing some benchmarking information that you will all benefit from. So long as information is shared on a

1   See, for example, www.goodcareguide.co.uk/childcare/nurseries, www.teachearlyyears.com/product-focus/view/rate-my-nursery, www.facebook.com/Ratemynursery.
2   www.reports.ofsted.gov.uk

reciprocal basis, i.e. I'll show you mine if you show me yours, then people are often happy to take part. (I was recently approached by someone in my own field of work who wanted to benchmark fee rates for different sorts of training courses. As a result of sharing my fees with them I received a really valuable report with anonymous data collected from a number of training providers and was able to determine whether I should change my fee rates in order to remain competitive.)

Mystery shopping – mystery shopping is a very commonly used way of conducting competitor research across a very wide range of sectors. Have you noticed sometimes, when you're in the supermarket, people walking round with clipboards taking notes. Often these are competitors checking how other retailers are marketing their products. And as a loyalty card holder I have been asked to act as a mystery shopper when using my local petrol station. I was sent a questionnaire to complete during my next visit asking about the level of service provided.

So there is nothing wrong with doing a bit of mystery shopping with your competitors. This could be as simple as looking online and trying to find information as if you were a parent, or calling them and asking the sort of questions that a prospective customer might ask. But could also involve visiting for a show around or even taking advantage of a taster session. It may not be appropriate for you as the setting manager to do the mystery shopping (you might be recognised by the staff at the competitor), but maybe one of your staff or a trusted customer could help you with this. I do recall one lady who attended my marketing course when they were thinking about opening a baby room telling me afterwards, 'I borrowed a baby for some mystery shopping'. I was a bit shocked until she explained that it was actually her sister's baby.

Choosing the right marketing methods to use

Once you have conducted some market research, you are then in a position to use that knowledge to plan the best ways to contact parents to let them know about your service. The methods you will select will differ depending on the target audience that you have identified for your marketing. Typically your marketing plan might include some of the following methods:

Marketing method	Consider using	Actions
Word of mouth	Current customers	Get your current customers involved in helping you to find other parents in similar situations to themselves.
	Other early years providers	Partner with other local providers who you might be able to work with to meet parents' needs, e.g. offering 30 hours provision by partnering with local childminders.
	Business networking, e.g. local Federation of Small Businesses, Chamber of Commerce meetings	Attract customers who work in or run local businesses.
	Social media	Get the word out generally that you have vacancies.
Top tip – Make it easy for them to pass on your details		
Get listed	Yellow Pages and other phone books	Get your free one line listing in Yellow Pages and negotiate hard if you decide to try out having a box advert or a Yell.com listing. If you go down this route take full advantage of their customer review facilities.
	Local newsletters and online portals	Ideal if you are targeting families in your local area. Many of these will offer a free or very low cost option for local businesses. Even quite small villages now have their own community webpage.
	Childcare registers, e.g. Family Information Service (FIS), Social Services	Find out how to get listed on any official lists maintained by your local authority or other government agencies. If you are able to provide special care, e.g. overnight, SEND (Special Educational Needs and Disabilities), emergency short term care you might find there are specific lists that you can ask to be included on.
	Local employers	The HR manager of larger local employers may be happy to share your details with parents who go to them to discuss their parental leave options. Be as helpful as you can by providing a nice information pack that they can give out.
	Social media groups	These could include Facebook groups focused on a specific location, groups linked with local schools or Children's Centres.
Top tip – Think carefully about the information that you want to share on various lists and how you will systematically update it when things change		

Marketing method	Consider using	Actions
Generate PR	Local papers and magazines – good news stories	As well as sending press releases about your good news and events, you could offer to write a regular column on caring for children.
	Sponsorship	Building a long-term relationship with local businesses can be useful, e.g., they might be happy to support you in exchange for some joint publicity.
	Open days/fetes and fun days	Having a physical presence at events attended by local families can be a nice way to get to know people face to face. Offer some sort of activity for the children to take part in at the event as a 'mini taster session' plus a voucher for any that subsequently contact you.
	Local radio	Most local radio stations cover and promote local community events and activities for free.
	Social media/blogs	Writing blogs where you share your ideas and tips is a great way of engaging with people who share your interests and building up a network of followers.
Top tip – Get good at writing press releases that your local press will be interested in		
Physical advertising	Shop windows/ notice boards	Advertising at a very local level is often very low cost, especially if you offer sessional care that is likely to be attractive to parents who use those shops.
	Local press adverts	Provides good local coverage but can be expensive.
	Leaflets and mail shots	Ideal to hand out to people who you meet at events, or to give to others to pass on for you. As noted earlier, targeted distribution of leaflets is essential to avoid wasting a lot of money.
	Signage	Alerting people to your physical location can be particularly important if your setting is tucked out of the way and not visible from the road, or if you want to attract parents who travel through your area. Signage can include buildings, street signs, car branding, children's uniforms etc.
	Information packs	Provide a professional image to parents and other professionals, e.g. HR managers and potential funders.
Top tip – Check who the audience is likely to be for each advert		

Digital advertising	Website	A low cost way of reaching a lot of people. If designed to be fully responsive it can be easily accessed using mobile devices. You can treat your website as an online brochure without printing and distribution costs, and with no impact on the environment.
	Direct email	Use of direct email is pretty much universal within the business community. It can be personalised.
	Social media platforms	Tailor different content to different platforms. This can enable you to reach a lot of people very easily. You could consider using paid-for adverts on social media sites (see below).
Top tip – Use digital tools to track and analyse statistics to demonstrate what works		

Attracting interest

Whichever marketing methods you decide you use, it's important to get the design and content right in order to make it attractive to prospective customers. So take some time to think about what works. If, for example, you plan to put a notice in your local shop window, go and stand in front of the window for a while and look at what's there currently. Ask yourselves these questions about what makes an advert appealing.

- Which ones stand out and catch your eye?

- What looks attractive?

- When you read them, what sounds attractive?

- What would make you want to call to find out more?

- How well do their differentiators come across?

- Which ones don't work and why?

Do the same for any other methods that you decide to use. For example, take the time to compare your competitors' websites with your own.

And don't just rely on your own opinion. Ask a couple of your existing parents for their opinions too.

Making your website work for you

Increasingly parents look online for information about childcare in their local area, and this is especially true of parents who are working. Making sure that people find your website when they search for information about childcare in your area is called Search Engine Optimisation (or SEO) – in other words making your website stand out to the search engines such as Google.

Search engine optimisation (SEO) is often marketed by IT consultants as some sort of mysterious dark art. Although it's not a quick fix, typically taking three to six months to start making an impact, it is something that can be handled by anyone who has access to a Content Management System (CMS) to manage the content of your website.

For each page of your website, complete metadata using a normal description (the few words of text that appear when your website appears as a result of a search). Google no longer uses keywords but some other search engines still do – match them to what people are likely to use as their search terms, for example, childcare in Brighton or nursery near Luton, etc. Some parents also use voice-activated search tools such as Siri or Cortana. This is changing the way we need to optimise webpages. If you do decide to use a consultant to do some of this for you, remember that SEO can be very expensive. So, set yourself a budget and make sure that you carefully evaluate what works for you before investing any more. Remember there are a lot of cowboys out there who can make you think that SEO is a dark art and will charge you a fortune to do things that are quite simple.

Good SEO can help you to get higher up when people search but you have to decide if it's worth the effort. Ultimately, the quality of what happens once people click on your website is much more important. Consistently creating quality content on your website so that people return to it again and again is the best way to become attractive to search engines. Blogs are a great way to create quality content. Add a blog section to your website and regularly write a short piece about some aspect of childcare that you think parents would be interested in reading. You could base it on the questions that parents have asked you over the past month, for example, how to support a child who is reluctant to talk, or on the experiences you have had with children in your setting recently, perhaps dealing with a child who bites. You could also share tips based on what you and your staff have learnt in recent training sessions. And remember, you don't have to do all the work yourself; it's fine to invite guest bloggers to contribute to your blog from time to time.

Another way to make your website valuable to visitors is to turn it into a resource centre for parents with young children. This might mean sharing some ideas that you have developed yourself or providing links to other sites that provide great resources. Ask parents to register before they can access this section of your website (again capturing their email address) and check from time to time that all the links you have included still work. Google provides a free Webmaster Tool to enable you to quickly and easily check your site for broken links.

It's also a good idea to include links to your own webpages as Google looks at the usability of your website and is interested to see how people can access different pages in a number of different ways. Adding links to your social media profiles, making them easy to access from your website is also helpful for SEO purposes.

And finally – and this may sound obvious – make sure your website name (URL) is shown on all of the other marketing materials that you produce.

Getting your key messages across

When you have chosen the method(s) that you are going to use to let your prospective customers know about your service, your next step is to consider the key messages that you need to get across. These need to be specific to your target customers and must cover the things that you have found out about them through your market research. Include in your marketing messages the things that your market research will have told you about what customers want and need, such as local provision that they can walk to, easy parking, a home from home environment, flexible hours, late opening times, etc.

Also include information about how you compare with other providers, highlighting benefits such as longer opening hours, more convenient location, higher staff ratios, specialist care for children with SEND requirements, etc. Make sure that you have a very clear understanding of what you have to offer customers that is special, that is different from your competitors, that makes your setting stand out from the rest. These things are what we call your differentiators or your USPs (unique selling points).

What's your plan?

Once you know who you are going to target, what they need and want, what methods you can use to make contact with them and what you need to say to attract them, you can put together a marketing plan which might look like this:

Activity	Objectives	Person responsible	Timescale	Costs	Success measures
What are you going to do? Examples might include: • Attend local fete • Hold open day • Update website to include blog	Examples might include: • To raise awareness of new services • To improve reputation within local community • To generate x new enquiries	Name someone in your business to be responsible for each activity	Break activities down into small steps and set yourself a deadline for each step	Include time as well as money	How will you judge whether it's been a success? This is important as it will tell you if it is an activity that's worth repeating

Harnessing the power of digital marketing (social media and more)

It is worth integrating the use of social media into your marketing plan because people tend to openly share a lot of information about themselves on social media. This means that you can build an in depth understanding and a strong relationship with them very easily. Social media is free and easy to use – you don't need to employ a consultant to use it. Increasingly it's mobile with over 71 per cent of people using apps on smartphones and tablets to access social media, so you can promote your services to people any time, any place, anywhere (Source: Adobe 2013 Mobile Consumer Survey).

Your various social media accounts can also be managed using third party apps such as Hootsuite or Tweetdeck, which offer many additional functions such as scheduling posts and tweets across multiple platforms, meaning that you don't have to be online yourself at 8pm in the evening in order to engage with people at that time. Social media puts small businesses on a level playing field with big businesses which have far more resources available to them. And don't forget that it is also great for easily keeping up to date with news and changes affecting your early years business, so it really is an essential part of your CPD.

Tips for using social media as part of your marketing plan

- Offer your Twitter followers or Facebook fans a taster session, a discount or special offer on a new service in exchange for giving you feedback about it to support its development – it makes them feel valued.

- Because you connect with people personally, this enables you to tailor your marketing to appeal to people personally – they may go on to become your customers, e.g., if you've engaged with them at the research stage of developing a new service.

- You can link the timing of promotional activity with changes that parents might have seen in the news, making your promotion feel highly relevant to them, e.g., government announcements about early years funding changes.

- If you're planning to expand your business geographically, social media can help you to begin to engage with people in a different location before you have a physical presence there.

- Social media can help you make use of the following activities as a part of your promotion of services:

  » Promotion of events

  » Driving traffic to your website or blog

  » Picking up ideas of things to blog about

  » Understanding the best time to promote your services, for example, linking it to a relevant Twitter Hour e.g., #EYTalking

» Things can go viral really easily if you get it right – think about #nomakeupselfies, #icebucketchallenge, #harveyandrabbit

» Raising awareness in people's minds about a need they didn't even know they had, e.g., how would you like childcare that works around your work schedule?

There are of course a few issues that you need to consider before getting involved in using social media as a promotional tool:

• If you are an active user of social media you will usually find that your Twitter account or your LinkedIn account comes at the top of a search of your name, so it's important to consider when you set your accounts up whether they should be in your own name or the name of your business.

• You can't control everything people say about you on social media, so you need to monitor all channels regularly for any negative comments made and respond to them – generally negative comments can be turned to your advantage if you respond appropriately, showing that you respond to customer feedback, apologise and then rectify any problems promptly. Avoid getting into a slanging match on social media – your aim is to promptly take the conversation offline.

• Once you put information out there using social media it can spread very quickly so it's essential to treat a Tweet or post as seriously as you would treat an expensive glossy brochure – spell-check it, make sure it's accurate and legal, make sure it's not offensive, etc.

• Social media is highly addictive – if you're not careful social media can take over your life, leaving no time to actually do your job and contributing to poor work-life balance, e.g., many Twitter Hours take place in the evenings or at weekends.

• If you use social media to build your reputation as an expert in your field it is essential to ensure that you really are and that you tweet/post about things that you know about – people will very quickly pick you up if you post something that is incorrect or inaccurate, thus damaging your reputation very publicly.

Social media and the law

Many of the considerations that apply to other forms of marketing also apply to using social media, for example, advertising standards. A few considerations are:

- Using social media to connect with and influence the behaviour of vulnerable people, including children, is highly unethical and runs the risk of inappropriate relationships (grooming) developing.

- Client confidentiality needs to be observed so, for example, tweeting that a particular parent has just bought a particular service is unacceptable.

- You also need to make sure that you're not breaching legal requirements about intellectual property, trademarks and copyright.

- Social media posts should not be offensive and should respect equality and diversity legislation.

Many small businesses find that using a range of social media platforms works for them. If you decide on this approach, consider using tools to help you to manage across multiple platforms such as Hootsuite or Tweet deck.

Here are a few thoughts about some of the different social media sites and how you might make use of them.

Twitter is ideal for:

- short pieces of information

- driving traffic to your website or blog by including a link (using a URL shortener)

- making initial contact

- beginning a conversation that can then be carried on using other means

- getting involved in a conversation using a hashtag, e.g. #EYTalking
- rapidly scanning for news and information
- engaging in Twitter Hours.

LinkedIn is ideal for:

- creating a professional profile page for your business (like an online business CV)
- linking with fellow professionals internationally both inside and outside of the EY sector
- building your reputation through Endorsements and Recommendations
- finding people with common interests to link with by using Groups
- setting up a public or private discussion forum for like-minded people by setting up your own Group.

Facebook is ideal for:

- creating both a personal profile and a business page, or a closed group for existing customers
- sharing information in more depth than you can on Twitter
- including photos and other images
- engaging with non-business customers who may not be familiar with other social networking sites.

Google+ is ideal for:

- enhancing your position within organic Google searches
- creating common interest groups using Circles
- participating in Google Hangouts to chat about a topic.

StreetLife is ideal for:

- raising awareness of your business locally as users follow a location rather than an individual
- promoting events such as open days or fundraising activities.

Instagram and *Pinterest* are ideal for:

- sharing photos of your setting so people can see what it looks like (take care about using photos showing children)

- businesses who want an online shop window (e.g., if you also sell products to parents)

- getting ideas and inspiration from what other people post about creative activities to do with children.

Blogs can also be considered social media and can easily be set up using WordPress. Blogs are ideal for:

- building your reputation as an expert

- creating a store of posts that you can recycle/repost

- quickly and easily sharing information and good news stories about your business – a blog post can be as short as you like – which provides an alternative to email and newsletters to parents

- linking to other social media sites (this process can be automated using a WordPress social media plug-in so that your blog automatically posts to your Facebook page or Twitter account) where readers are likely to share your posts giving a positive impression to prospective parents

- improving search engine optimisation (SEO) – this makes it easier for prospective customers to find you when they search for childcare in your area

- encouraging people to visit the rest of your website and to become repeat visitors to your website (if your blogs are interesting people will keep coming back for more) so that you build and develop your relationship with them

- engaging with people by inviting them to comment on your blog posts (but make sure that you have the power to vet comments before they are posted live).

An ideal blog post shouldn't be too long. It should seek to inform, educate, entertain or inspire rather than sell. It should be well-written using correct spelling, grammar and punctuation, and well structured using:

- headings and subheadings

- bulleted or numbered lists

- visual graphics such as diagrams, graphs, photos and videos

- quotes that personalise the message

- clear call-to-action buttons or messages about what the reader should do next.

Paying to advertise on social media

Any social media advert needs to be consistent with your brand and with any other advertising and marketing that you might do, so that customers are not confused and so that your overall reputation is enhanced by the advert.

Before you invest money in creating social media site adverts, it is essential to conduct some market research in order to determine the likely response of your potential customers to such an approach. Market research could include phoning some existing customers and asking them, or looking at what your competitors are doing. This can help you to decide which social media platform to use and the type of content to include in your advert in order to maximise its reach. As with any other campaign, selecting your target audience/ segmentation is important.

Once you have decided to try out a social media site advert you need to consider the cost. Most sites will allow you to set up a low cost campaign where you can limit the amount of money to be invested. So, in order to test it out, you could specify that you only want to spend £50.

You should also consider the timing of the advert. Vary the time of day, day of the week, time of year depending on the message you want to get across and who you are hoping to target. Working parents, for example, tend to use social media in the evenings after the children are in bed.

Good images tend to improve the reach of social media adverts as well as good content, so identifying a source of good quality, low cost stock images is useful. Some platforms such as Facebook provide access to these when you set an advert up. Making sure that images comply with the rules of that platform is important, for example less than 20 per cent text for images in a Facebook advert.

Limitations of social media

Despite the advantages outlined above, there are certain limitations imposed by using social media sites for promotional campaigns. It is important to read the terms and conditions of use of each social media site that you use to ensure you comply with their requirements and restrictions. Specific platforms also have specific limitations, for example:

- Twitter has a limit of 140 characters per Tweet, doesn't allow you to select people to target or to target groups of people at once and doesn't allow you to send the same message out repeatedly

- Facebook doesn't allow you to use images with more than 20 per cent text.

Advertising on a social networking site is subject to the same legal standards as any other form of marketing. This includes legislation such as:

- Advertising Standards[3]

- The Trades Description Act 1968[4]

- Distance Selling Regulations[5]

- The Sale of Goods Act 1979.[6]

In addition you need to ensure you observe and respect copyright and intellectual property by seeking permission where necessary, and referencing any source materials referred to.

Other issues to consider might include the following:

- Some people are wary about being marketed to in this way and so may not feel positively about your business for using this method.

- Certain customers might not use the internet or may still have very limited broadband, making it difficult for them to access certain types of content such as photographs and video.

---

3   www.asa.org.uk/Consumers/What-we-cover.aspx?gclid=CNrS1vT628ECFc
Tnwgod8hUAag
4   www.legislation.gov.uk/ukpga/1968/29
5   www.gov.uk/online-and-distance-selling-for-businesses/overview
6   www.legislation.gov.uk/ukpga/1979/54

- It doesn't replace human interaction – in many businesses (especially in the service sector) people buy people and the personal face to face touch is important.

- It should always be remembered that this is not the only method to run a promotional campaign.

- Reputation can take a long time to build but only seconds to destroy; remember the Gerald Ratner story I told earlier. The following factors are likely to cause negative reactions, so make sure you avoid them:

  » Exaggerating claims about the benefits of your services

  » Poor spelling and grammar

  » Being too pushy and hard selling

  » Promoting something you can't deliver

  » Divulging confidential information either intentionally or inadvertently

  » Making political comments/ranting

  » Using bad language

  » Posting on the wrong page (if you manage several different pages)

  » Criticising your competitors.

Measuring what works

It's essential to evaluate the effectiveness of any form of marketing. This is important in order to avoid wasting resources on marketing activity that doesn't achieve anything for your business, or investing too heavily in activity where the return on investment is minimal.

This means being clear up front what you expect each activity to do for your business. This could include things like:

- I want to create general awareness (you could ask parents if they know you exist?)

- I want to raise awareness of a new service (you could ask parents if they know you now offer...?)

- I want to direct people to my website (check click through rates)

- I want to generate new enquiries (ask anyone who contacts you where they found out about you).

The results achieved need to be weighed up against the resources (time, effort, money) that have to be invested to achieve those results by conducting a cost/benefit analysis. Without having defined the desired outcomes it is not possible to undertake this sort of evaluation and you risk wasting resources on marketing activity that doesn't deliver a reasonable level of results.

You could even try running the same adverts in parallel at the same times using different marketing methods in order to figure out which ones work best for you.

Monitoring the effectiveness of digital advertising

If you use digital platforms to market your business, results can be monitored quite easily through tools provided by those platforms. These tools provide extensive information about how people have engaged with your messages.

- *Google Analytics* can be used to report on data about the behaviour of visitors to your website including:

  » how visitors found your site (including the search terms that they used)

  » whether they have clicked through from somewhere else, e.g. a social media post

  » where they are located

  » which pages they visited

  » what time/day they visited

  » how long they spent on each page

  » what type of device they used to view your site.

- *Facebook Insights* tells you about visitors to your Facebook page including:
  - » what time/day people visited
  - » which posts were most widely shared (referred to as reach)
  - » how many Likes you received
  - » the location of your Fans as well as their gender and age.
- *Twitter Analytics* tells you about:
  - » impressions (number of times users saw your Tweet)
  - » engagement rates including:
    - – link clicks
    - – retweets
    - – favourites
    - – replies.
- *LinkedIn* allows you to:
  - » ask customers for endorsements and recommendations (testimonials)
  - » categorise your connections, e.g. existing customers, competitors, prospective customers, etc.

If your monitoring and evaluation demonstrate that your marketing is not delivering the results you had hoped for you might need to:

- review and amend your objectives ensuring they are more specific and achievable
- conduct further market research to build your understanding of your target audience
- invest more money to allow it to make more of an impact
- alter the timing of the campaign
- redesign your marketing materials using different content, better quality images, and correct any errors

- use a different marketing method

- acknowledge that the methods you are using may not be suitable for what you are trying to achieve – in which case stop doing it.

Retaining customers by managing relationships with parents

It is less costly to retain existing customers because you don't have to go through the process of finding them, conducting research, understanding their needs from scratch, getting to know them, etc.

Existing customers also provide an immediate target audience for new services that you might be thinking about introducing. They can also be invited to 'market test' new services before they are formally launched to a wider audience.

Loyal customers make the very best ambassadors for your business. Asking them to provide reviews and testimonials and to act as advocates for your early years business by talking to other parents not only provides trustworthy information to potential new customers, but also cements your relationship with them. Asking them to say nice things about your setting reminds them that they love you and will prompt them to stay with you come what may.

Particularly in the digital age, potential customers will often place more trust in customer reviews and testimonials than they will in any marketing communications produced by the business itself.

So let's think about how to turn your existing customers into 'raving fans' who will happily, and without prompting, tell people how great your setting is. Ken Blanchard (1993, pp.101, 123) says in his book *Raving Fans*, 'Discover what the customer wants' then 'deliver the vision plus one percent'. He goes on to say 'Customers have needs beyond the need of the…particular service. People need to feel they belong... People need to feel that they're important and that what they do, think, and say truly matters.'

So the first step in turning your customers into a fan club of raving fans for your setting is to understand what they want – what they really, really want.

Understanding parents' expectations

As human beings when we decide to buy something we are making a whole series of quite complex decisions – do I want it, do I need it, can I afford it, etc. This is true of anything that we buy, but is far more complex when we are making the decision to buy a service rather than a product in a box on a shelf. With a product, the decision is quite transactional (does it do what I need it to do), but with a service there is often a lot more emotional stuff going on behind the scenes which influences our decision making. And the more personal or intimate the service, the more important the emotional factors become.

Think how true this is in respect of some of the services that you buy. How does your decision making process differ if you are buying a new tyre for your car compared with the decision to book an appointment with a new hairdresser? What would you think about before making each of those buying decisions? How would you feel just before committing to the decision?

I hope this illustrates my point. Making a decision to buy a service is more complex and more emotionally charged than buying an object.

Now I'd like to you think about how you felt once you had made the decision and realised that it was a good decision. How do you feel after buying your new tyre compared with how you feel when you walk out of the hairdressers and catch sight of yourself in a shop window or a mirror?

Again I suspect that our responses to being a satisfied customer feel quite different when it is the intimate service that we are thinking about.

Finally using the same example, how would you feel if you were told that your usual tyres were going to be a lot more expensive. You'd probably just shop around for cheaper ones. But what if your wonderful hairdresser tells you that she's increasing her prices? I'm guessing that, like me, you'd probably find this quite stressful and make every effort to continue to use their services. Going out of your way to use a particular service is part of what raving fans do, as opposed to mere customers.

So, finding out what parents really, really want, what really matters to them, is your first step. And this doesn't mean just sending them a survey and asking them to tick a few boxes while their giving the children their tea or watching a TV programme. This requires a commitment to taking time to make them feel they belong, to make them feel important, to make sure they know that what they do, think, and say truly matters.

So, perhaps once a year, invite parents in to sit down with you, to share a cuppa and a cake, and to chat about what really matters to them.

Creating a Parent Charter to manage their expectations

Once you have developed a clear picture of what your customers really, really want, you might consider capturing this in a Parent Charter which sets out clearly what parents can expect from you. Not only does this help to cement your relationship with your existing customers by showing them that you've listened to them, but it also helps you to send clear messages to prospective customers, to train your staff on what's expected of them and to provide great evidence in your Self Evaluation Form (SEF) of the way in which you engage parents as partners. There are some really nice examples from other industries – just search for good examples of customers' charters and take a look. I particularly like the EasyJet one.[7]

Measuring parent satisfaction

Your final step is then to measure how well your customers think you are doing in terms of living up to your Charter promises. As suggested previously, survey your customers from time to time and publish the results on a 'You said... We did...' section on your website and in your other marketing communications.

---

7   www.easyjet.com/en/orange-spirit/our-promise

Chapter 6

RECRUITING, MANAGING AND DEVELOPING EMPLOYEES AND VOLUNTEERS

The people section of your Early Years Business Dashboard is the next thing that I'd like to address. This chapter focuses on sharing some recognised good practice in relation to the recruitment, management and development of staff and (as many settings work with them) volunteers. I don't intend to cover everything you need to know about this subject, because it is a huge area that would merit a separate book in its own right, and many other publications already cover many of these areas fully. So, for example, I won't attempt to create a section on Safer Recruitment within Early Years. Rather, I will focus on the areas that typically I find my early years clients find challenging and where they most often address things in a way that might fall foul of the law. I will cover a balance between general principles and legal compliance, and provide a number of good practice checklists, as well as signposting you to helpful and reliable sources of help, support and information.

A word of warning!

I begin all my employment law workshops with the story of a lady who attended one of my courses and proudly announced at the start of the day that she had all her policies in place and that she'd had someone advise her when she started up her setting. I applauded this to the rest of the group as good practice. However, as the day went on she started to say a few things that concerned me so I quizzed her a bit about the person who had advised her. It turns out that it was the husband of a member of their committee. I asked what his professional status was and she said, 'He's a very successful businessman running a local minicab business – he employs loads of staff and really knows how to run a business!' Unfortunately I had to advise her that some of the things that she'd put in place were inappropriate for her business – and some were positively illegal! So the lesson here is: if you need legal advice, find a lawyer – not a mate who says he knows a bit about the law!

Added to that story, here is my word of warning. You are not an Employment Lawyer – and neither am I – don't be tempted to dabble in things that you are not qualified to deal with. So, although I am a qualified HR practitioner, there comes a point where I often have to say to my clients, 'I'm sorry I can't help you with that – you need to take legal advice'. Business and employment law is complex and subject to constant changes – never assume that because something was right on a previous occasion that it will still be so – always check with reliable sources for up to date legal information.

So, for the purposes of this book, the information provided does not constitute legal advice for your business and was correct at the time of going to press, but may have changed since. If you have an issue that you need to address, you should speak to an appropriately qualified adviser who can advise you on your specific situation and on the law as it currently stands. This doesn't need to cost you a fotunre (it is likely that your insurance company and/or trade organisation provides a legal helpline as part of a deal you have with them) and will save you a lot of heartache (and potentially money) in the long run.

A word about Brexit

At the time of writing this book, the UK government is faced with putting into effect the UK's exit from the EU following the referendum result in June 2016.

The Brexit vote has created uncertainty in many aspects of our lives, and how it will affect HR and employment law is one of those that many early years businesses are wondering and worrying about. For many who voted to leave the EU, it was the imposition of EU red tape and regulations that perhaps prompted that vote. And it would be true to say that some of the UK's employment legislation does have its origins in Brussels. This includes areas such as:

- anti-discrimination

- treatment of pregnant workers

- working time rights

- employment of agency workers

- rights to collective consultation

- health and safety rights.

However, the process that our government has used over many years is to weave various pieces of EU legislation into the UK's own legislation rather than tag it on the side. An example of this would be laws relating to equality and discrimination. In 2010 the UK government removed a whole host of our existing legislation and replaced those laws with the Equality Act. This incorporates both EU and UK legislation in one Act.

And in some cases the UK government has taken things further than required by the EU and has introduced legislation that goes beyond the original EU requirements.

Although the Brexit vote does mean that the UK government will no longer be constrained by EU rules, if they do wish to remove certain pieces of legislation in an effort to reduce red tape for businesses, those laws will then be reviewed and amended over a period of many years, as and when Parliament has the will and time to review them. The government also has to consider that those businesses who wish to continue trading with the EU may find that future trade agreements still require them to demonstrate that they are meeting EU standards in order to continue with that trade relationship (this is unlikely to be an issue for the early years and childcare sector but is certainly a consideration for the government when they think about how to adapt our labour laws).

So in summary:

- Nothing will change any time soon – radical changes are likely to take many years.

- Changes may not be as radical as some might be expecting – whole chunks of legislation are unlikely simply to disappear – changes are likely to be minor and implemented in a piecemeal fashion as each individual piece of legislation is reviewed.

- Businesses may still need to abide by certain EU rules if they wish to trade with the EU.

My key message to employers in the early years sector at this time is – keep calm and carry on!

Recruitment challenges

I'm going to cover a couple of the areas where I find that early years businesses are often at risk of falling foul of the law when taking on new staff.

Avoiding discrimination when recruiting staff

The Equality Act 2010 replaced a whole raft of existing discrimination laws, bringing them all together under one piece of legislation. It aimed to make discrimination legislation more consistent, clearer and easier to follow.

The Act covers all aspects of employment, including the recruitment process, terms and conditions, benefits, and opportunities for promotion and training. It also covers unfair treatment compared to other workers, and such issues as dismissal, harassment and victimisation.

The Act defines nine protected characteristics: age, disability, gender reassignment, marriage and civil partnership, pregnancy and maternity, race, religion or belief, gender and sexual orientation. These protected characteristics must be considered carefully in any decisions that are made affecting your staff.

The recruitment process is one of those times when settings most frequently run the risk of behaving in a way that could be considered discriminatory.

There are a few simple steps that you can take to avoid this risk:

- check adverts are fair – steer clear of any reference to protected characteristics to avoid discrimination in job adverts; phrases such as 'mature person', 'recent graduate' or 'ten years' experience' are potentially discriminatory

- avoid bias – where only one person makes the decision, there is the possibility of bias creeping in so, where possible, have more than one person involved

- train interviewers – everyone who is involved at any stage of the selection process, such as short-listing or interviewing, should be trained or well briefed on how to avoid discriminatory behaviour – this includes committee members within committee-run settings

- have a consistent process – a pre-planned interview process which ensures every candidate is asked the same questions will make sure you are fair to everyone, but remember that you may also need to ask follow-up questions based on their replies so your interviewers need to be capable of doing that in a non-discriminatory way

- competency-based – basing your selection process on a list of the competencies that you need the person to be able to demonstrate will keep you focused on their ability rather than their personal characteristics; draw up a person specification focusing on skills and knowledge, experience, aptitudes, qualifications and personal qualities, spelling out which are essential and which are desirable

- include activities to test – reliance on an interview as your only method for selecting people can lead to subjective decisions being made that could be difficult to justify if challenged; consider how you could test if a candidate has the competencies you require by building other activities into your selection process

- take care with social media – many organisations routinely check people's social media profiles as a part of the recruitment process, however be aware that this might reveal things such as a disability and lead to discriminatory judgments

- practise safer recruitment – the practices that you should be following in order to keep children safe will also support you, e.g., asking candidates to complete a standard application form rather than submitting a CV makes the process fairer for all – but take care when drawing up your application form, e.g., asking for a form to be filled out 'in your own handwriting' may discriminate against people with dyslexia; do not ask for details related to protected characteristics such as date and place of birth, marital status or health absence details.

How to avoid discrimination during the recruitment process

One of the situations when we are most at risk of discriminatory practice in respect of a disability is when we are recruiting new staff.

You can't ask questions about a candidate's health during the recruitment process. This includes asking whether or not a candidate has a disability. You can only ask someone about their medical circumstances after they have been offered the job. If, on the basis of this information, you then withdraw the job offer you will need to make sure that it is on a non-discriminatory basis. This includes considering any reasonable adjustments that could be made to allow the person to take up the post.

It is still acceptable to ask questions about a person's health for the following purposes:

- equality monitoring – questions about candidates' gender, ethnicity, disability etc. should be asked on a form which is kept separate from the application form and only looked at once the employment offer has been made

- to conduct positive action such as changing the date of a job interview if it coincides with a medical appointment

- to enquire whether reasonable adjustments are needed so that they can take part in the recruitment process, e.g. a downstairs room for the interview

- to establish whether the job applicant will be able to carry out a function that is *fundamental* to the role, e.g., if your job vacancy requires them to be able to pick up and carry a disabled child you have the right to find out if a health condition could prevent a candidate from carrying out that task.

And finally, keep records showing clearly how the decision to appoint the successful candidate was reached. This includes any notes made by interviewers which candidates can ask to see afterwards. So I always warn interviewers not to write anything down that they wouldn't feel happy about the candidate reading.

Employing people you shouldn't

There are two main issues to consider here: the risk of employing someone who isn't allowed to work here (this could well change over the coming years post-Brexit), and the risk of employing someone who isn't allowed to work with children. I'm not going to cover the requirements defined under the Safer Recruitment rules in respect of Enhanced DBS Checks and other safeguarding checks that you need to conduct. If you are unsure of your obligations here check out the government regulations on Safeguarding Children.

The Immigration, Asylum and Nationality Act 2006 sets out clearly which overseas nationals are permitted to work in the UK, the checks that you must undertake before employing someone and the paperwork required to demonstrate compliance. This was updated by the Immigration Act 2016.

This is important because the penalties for businesses that get it wrong (even unintentionally) are severe. Knowingly employing someone who doesn't have permission to work here, including where there is 'reasonable cause to believe that the person has no right to do the work' is viewed as a criminal offence that carries an unlimited fine or up to five years' imprisonment. Employers who fail to conduct thorough checks, or to keep copies of documentary evidence of such checks, can be subject to civil prosecution and a maximum fine of £20,000 per illegal worker. In these cases the employer and/or the individual manager who is responsible for the recruitment decision can both be prosecuted.[1]

To ensure that you do not discriminate against anyone, you should conduct right to work checks on all potential employees. You should not make assumptions about a person's right to work in the UK or their immigration status on the basis of their name, skin colour, nationality, ethnic or national origins, dress, accent or length of time they have been resident in the UK.

There are three basic steps that you should follow:

---

1   You can find the statutory process to be followed with an online tool at www.gov.uk/guidance/new-employee-coming-to-work-from-abroad and the Home Office has produced a very useful guide for employers www.gov.uk/government/uploads/system/uploads/attachment_data/file/536953/An_Employer_s_guide_to_right_to_work_checks_-_July_16.pdf.

- *obtain* original versions of one or more acceptable documents

- *check* the document's validity in the presence of the holder

- *copy* the document, record the date the check was made and keep the copy safe.

A particular occasion where a risk occurs is when your setting merges with or takes over another setting, and staff from that setting become the employees of your setting under a TUPE transfer. It is tempting to assume that all appropriate checks were carried out when they were originally employed; however, it is not safe to do so. As the new employer you carry the legal responsibility to undertake full checks and you should do this as a part of your due diligence checks while going through the process. The law now allows you 60 days to carry out 'right to work' checks.

Challenges when contracting with employees

There are a few issues that should be carefully thought through when drawing up an offer and a contract of employment.

Inappropriate use of self-employed contracts

In October 2016 HMRC announced that they planned to crack down on businesses that use self-employed contracts as a way of reducing their tax burden. They believe that up to half a million people may be wrongfully classed as self-employed by their employers, denying them protections such as maternity pay and pensions, at a cost to the Treasury of £300 million in lost National Insurance contributions.

And yet in spite of this, I had a very worrying conversation recently about early years settings that are contracting with their staff on a self-employed basis and assume this is just a matter of choice. I have also come across childminders who are expanding and taking on an assistant but who employ their assistants on a self-employed basis. The people I was speaking with about this were not aware that HMRC has very strict criteria which they use to determine whether an individual can be classified as self-employed, and that to fail to employ someone and pay them through the PAYE system is a serious offence.

The HMRC website provides a simple checklist that employers can use to determine whether someone working for them is classed as employed or self-employed.[2] In almost all cases, in our sector, staff would fail to pass the test that classifies them as self-employed on several counts.

A worker can be classified as self-employed if they:

- are in business for themselves, are responsible for the success or failure of their business and can make a loss or a profit

- can decide what work they do and when, where or how to do it

- can hire someone else to do the work (sub-contracting)

- are responsible for fixing any unsatisfactory work in their own time

- have agreed a fixed price for their work – it doesn't depend on how long the job takes to finish

- use their own money to buy business assets, cover running costs, and provide tools and equipment for their work

- can work for more than one client.

Making use of probation periods

You are legally required to provide every employee with a written statement of employment particulars (often referred to as a contract of employment) within two months of employing them. Failure to do so can result in an Employment Tribunal, and could require you to pay compensation to the employee.

When you appoint a new staff member, the hope is that you've made the right decision; however, there's always a chance that they may turn out to be not be the right person for the role, or not to fit well within your existing team.

Offering a contract which contains a probation period is essential to allow you to more easily make the hard decision to dismiss them. It allows you to set a shorter notice period, for example, one week which means that if a staff member clearly isn't right for your

---

2   www.hmrc.gov.uk/employment-status/#1

business they can be dismissed and exited quickly. A probation period also provides a great opportunity for you to monitor their performance and make sure that their induction into your setting is going smoothly.

It's entirely up to you how long a probation period lasts for, and also whether it can be extended. This must be written into the contract. Most employers settle with either three or six months (depending on the role). At that point a formal review should take place, confirming whether the employee has met the requirements (in which case their position is confirmed as permanent) or not.

So what do you do if their performance hasn't been acceptable? You can either dismiss them or take the decision to extend their probation period to allow them an opportunity to improve. I have lots of conversations with clients about extending a staff member's probation period and often the conversation revolves around the employee promising to improve and the employer wanting to give them another chance. But what you do need to consider carefully is the reasons why they have failed to meet the requirements of the job:

- *Lack of competence* – if this is the case, consider if you have provided appropriate induction training and management support

- *Lack of capability* – if this is the case, consider if they may have a disability which requires you to make reasonable adjustments to enable them to fulfil the role requirements

- *Poor attitude* – if this is the case, consider if you have fed back to them alerting them to your concerns and giving them an opportunity to improve

- *Inappropriate behaviour* – if this is the case, consider the seriousness and whether their behaviour constitutes misconduct.

Ask yourself the question – if they're not the right person for the job after three months, are they likely to become so after four months, or five months or six? A decision to extend a probation period can often result in a lot of additional stress managing an under-performing employee, and requires the same tough decision to be made in the long run anyway.

Good practice would be to make sure that you don't leave it until the end of the probation period to have a conversation with the employee about their poor performance. This conversation should take place on an ongoing basis throughout the probation period so that the formal review at (or before) the end of the probation period simply confirms what they already know, i.e., that they are under-performing. But at the end of the day remember that, provided you don't dismiss them for an automatically unfair reason, e.g. because they are pregnant or have a disability, then you can dismiss them within the first two years of their employment without any risk of them bringing a case for unfair dismissal.

Getting the day to day stuff right

Next, I will explore a few of the day to day challenges that you might need to give some thought to as an employer.

Failure to pay National Minimum Wage (NMW)

Over the past few years we have become accustomed to operating in an environment where a rate of National Minimum Wage (NMW) is set by the government, and is reviewed and increased each year. This now includes a National Living Wage for older employees.

Yet despite the fact that the NMW has been with us since 1999, and that there are penalties in place to fine employers who fall foul of the law, there are still many occasions when employers either deliberately or inadvertently fail to pay their staff in accordance with the NMW. This has become such a concern that the UK government recently began a process of publicly 'naming and shaming' those employers who they have identified as failing to pay NMW. A list is produced quarterly and I am always disappointed to read when it includes early years providers.

I guess that this is perhaps inevitable in a sector where typically pay is low and many staff are employed on rates at or close to NMW. We also work in a sector where part time and flexible working is common and, in most cases, it is complications that arise from calculating pay for staff with complex working patterns that lead to failures to pay NMW.

The rules regarding the NMW are quite clear but can be complicated to apply. If you manage your own payroll you might want to check with your own advisers or with ACAS to make sure you've got it right.[3]

Paying the right holiday pay

This is another area where I find early years businesses often get into a muddle. First of all, let's look at the basics that are laid down by law. Paid holidays are statutory for all staff in the UK. The current requirement is for a full time employee to be paid for 5.6 weeks holiday per annum (equivalent to 28 days including the eight public holidays). Part time employees are entitled to the same amount of holiday as full time colleagues but calculated on a pro-rata basis. So if they work a three day week, the entitlement is 16.8 days leave. Additional annual leave (either paid or unpaid) may be agreed as part of an employee's contract. An employee's holiday entitlement must be included in their contract of employment.

So let's move on to consider a few of the complications and pitfalls that often cause confusion for early years employers.

Employers can specify the times when employees can take their leave, for example, only during the school holidays. Holiday pay should always be paid during the month when the holiday is actually taken meaning that you should run your payroll during August, paying your staff their holiday pay for that month, rather than rolling holiday pay up into their salary through the rest of the year, a practice that many term time only settings have typically used. If you do decide to roll their holiday pay up into their term-time salary, it is essential that you itemise this in their contract and on their payslips as a rate for hour and a rate in lieu of holiday pay. It is also essential that you ensure that they do actually take adequate holiday time – paid holidays are a legal entitlement from a health and wellbeing point of view as people need time to rest.

Employees must take at least four weeks of statutory leave during the leave year, but may carry over up to eight days of any remaining time off with your agreement. They can only be paid in lieu for this if their employment with you ends. If their employment ends, they

---

3   www.acas.org.uk/index.aspx?articleid=1902

have the right to be paid for any leave due but not taken, in addition to any pay in lieu of notice, etc.

There is no legal right to paid time off on the actual day of a public holiday. So if for some reason your setting is open on the day of a public holiday and this is a normal day of work for employees, they can't demand the day off. This is unlikely to happen in our sector but happens often in industries such as catering and hospitality, or public services like hospitals which continue to operate on those days.

There are different rules for calculating holiday pay depending on the working patterns involved. Here are a few examples:

- If an employee has no 'normal' working hours, because you have agreed a flexible contract such as a zero hours contract with them, then their holiday entitlement and pay would usually be calculated by working out the average pay received over the previous 12 weeks in which they were paid.

- A part-time employee who normally works on Mondays would be treated in respect of Bank Holidays to someone who never works on a Monday.

- Guaranteed and normal non-guaranteed overtime,[4] where there is no obligation by the employer to offer overtime but, if they do, then the employee is obliged by their contract to work overtime, should be taken into account when calculating an employee's statutory holiday pay entitlement. There is currently no definitive case law that suggests voluntary overtime needs to be taken into account, but this could change in the future.

- Work-related travel,[5] for example, a manager who travels to different settings within a nursery group, may need to be taken into account when calculating statutory holiday pay if payments are made for time spent travelling.

- Employees who are off sick or are taking parental leave, continue to accrue annual leave and holiday pay. You must allow an employee to carry over a maximum of 20 days if

---

4   See www.acas.org.uk/index.aspx?articleid=4109
5   See www.acas.org.uk/index.aspx?articleid=4109#work-related-travel

they are on long term sick leave and therefore unable to take their leave within the year.

Employing agency staff

Under the Agency Workers (Amendment) regulations 2011, agency staff are entitled to certain employment rights. This will apply to your early years business if you employ temporary staff through an agency for the purposes of cover. If you have built up your own bank of temporary staff that you recruit and employ directly then the rules don't apply.

Agency staff are, of course, entitled to the National Minimum Wage, paid annual leave, rest breaks and limits on working time, and access to benefits such as discounted childcare (if this is provided to comparable employees). They must also be kept informed about job vacancies.

However, the regulations also give agency staff the entitlement to the same, or no less favourable, treatment as comparable employees with respect to basic employment and working conditions, once they have completed a qualifying period of 12 continuous weeks in a particular job. This may include pay and holiday pay. It does not include redundancy pay, contractual sick pay, and maternity, paternity or adoption pay. Agency staff will also be entitled to paid time off to attend ante-natal appointments during their working hours.

Be warned – the regulations contain anti-avoidance measures, with significant fines if you try to get around the 12 week rule by ending employment and then re-employing the person.

Snow days and slow days

I've called this section snow days but actually it applies to any situation where you have made the decision (either willingly or by force) to close your setting. Other examples that I encounter from time to time are settings based in village halls that are required to close in order to be used as polling stations, and settings that have been forced to close following a serious health and safety incident or a failure in utilities. It's imperative that you have a clear policy so that staff know what you expect from them in terms of getting to work and being paid in these situations.

If you decide to remain open during bad weather, staff are not automatically entitled to pay if they are unable to get to work. However, do consider the health and safety implications of insisting that a staff member drives to work in potentially hazardous driving conditions. Just because the conditions are driveable where you are, doesn't mean to say that it is the same where they live.

If you close your setting and your staff are still able to report for work, you may still be obliged to pay them. It is not safe to rely on 'custom and practice' in these situations (for example, saying 'well we never pay staff if we decide we can't open due to snow').

What determines how staff are treated in these situations is what is written into their contract and/or your staff handbooks. A Lay-off Clause can be included in your contract which allows you to ask staff not to come to work if you need to close (or if you have insufficient work for them to do). This should state clearly that they won't get paid in those circumstances.

Avoiding discrimination

The Equality Act also defined a number of ways in which discrimination can occur, which I have described below with an example of each:

Direct discrimination occurs where a person receives poor treatment because of a protected characteristic compared to someone who does not have that characteristic. Some examples include:

- You turn down a staff member's application for promotion to a team leader position because you know that some of the parents who she would have to deal with are homophobic, and the staff member is open about being a lesbian. (Protected characteristic: sexual orientation.)

- You decide not to promote a staff member because she has told you that she has dyslexia and you feel that she wouldn't be able to cope with the amount of paperwork required by the more senior role. (Protected characteristic: disability.)

- A management vacancy has come up in your setting and a number of internal staff apply. One employee matches the job description more closely than the other applicants but you decide the more senior role wouldn't suit her because she is quite young and you're concerned that other staff members wouldn't take her seriously. (Protected characteristic: age.)

Indirect discrimination occurs when there is a rule, policy or practice that applies to everyone, but which disadvantages people with a particular protected characteristic compared to people without that characteristic. Some examples include:

- You have to make redundancies and have decided to select people who should be made redundant based on the amount of sick leave they have taken over the past 12 months. (Protected characteristic: disability.)

- A staff member has asked you to allow her to take her lunch break at your busiest time of the day so that she can take her medication, which she has to take with food. You tell her she can't do this as it would disrupt your rotas. (Protected characteristic: disability.)

- At the end of the year you decide to award bottles of champagne to any team members who have excelled during the year. No alternative non-alcoholic prize is made available to Muslim team members. (Protected characteristic: religion.)

Harassment includes any behaviour towards a person with a protected characteristic that they find offensive, frightening, degrading, humiliating or in any way distressing. Some examples include:

- An angry parent shouts at a Polish staff member saying, 'I wish you lot would hurry up and go back to your own country'. Although she is upset by this, you calm her down and tell her not to take it personally. Nothing is said to the parent as you don't want them to get angry again. (Protected characteristic: race.)

- A staff member has disclosed to you that she has been diagnosed with a mental health disability. She's embarrassed about having a mental illness and doesn't want her colleagues to know. You are concerned about how she is coping so you make a point of popping into the room from time to time and asking her if she is feeling alright. Her colleagues quiz her about why you keep asking if she's ok. (Protected characteristic: disability.)

- A Muslim staff member who wears a hijab is told by her colleagues that she should stop wearing it because it makes her look like a terrorist. Everyone laughs at the joke because she's obviously not a terrorist. (Protected characteristic: religion.)

Victimisation occurs when a person with a protected characteristic is treated less favourably than other employees because they have attempted to assert their rights. Some examples include:

- A manager is being difficult about an employee's request for time off for appointments with their diabetes counsellor. The employee reports the problem to the Committee, who tell the manager that they must let the employee have the time off. The manager is angry that the employee went 'over her head' to the Committee and as a result gives them a poor appraisal branding them 'a negative moaner'. (Protected characteristic: disability.)

- A staff member provides a witness statement in support of a colleague who has raised a grievance about homophobic bullying at work. A few months later they apply for a promotion but you turn them down (although they have the necessary skills and experience) because you feel they are a trouble-maker and have shown disloyalty to the business. (Protected characteristic: sexual orientation,)

Discrimination by association occurs if a person experiences discrimination because they are associated with someone who has a protected characteristic, such as their partner or child. Some examples include:

- A woman that you employ has taken a lot of time off while her husband has been undergoing treatment for MS. You decide to take disciplinary action against her. (Protected characteristic: disability.)

- You decide not to promote a staff member because their partner has recently been diagnosed with cancer and you are concerned that they would be unable to give sufficient attention to their job. (Protected characteristic: disability.)

Discrimination by perception occurs where a person is discriminated against because someone thinks they have one of the protected characteristics. For example:

- You reject a job candidate's application because they have a Chinese-sounding name and you wish to avoid the complications involved in employing a non-EU national. As it happens the candidate was born in the UK and is a UK citizen. (Protected characteristic: race.)

How to avoid disability discrimination

You have a duty to make 'reasonable adjustments' to your workplace and working practices to ensure that people with a disability are not put at a disadvantage compared to others. There is no fixed definition of what is 'reasonable'. What is reasonable will depend on all the circumstances, including practicality, cost, and the extent to which your business would be disrupted by any adjustments required.

Reasonable adjustments for an employee with a disability might include things like:

- letting them take time off to attend medical appointments

- modifying their job description to remove tasks that cause particular difficulty, either temporarily or permanently, for example, lifting babies

- being flexible around working hours, perhaps allowing a later start so they can avoid busy public transport

- allowing extra breaks to help them cope with fatigue

- adjusting performance targets, for example, the number of key children to be supported and reported on, to take into account the effect of sick leave/fatigue, etc.

- moving their working location to another room, e.g., to avoid stairs

- ensuring easy access to premises for someone who is using a wheelchair or crutches, or who is partially sighted

- providing disabled toilet facilities

- allowing a gradual, phased return to work after extended sick leave.

Any planned adjustments should be discussed with, and approved by, the employee concerned.

Remember always that actions you take or decisions you make will be lawful if they can be justified as meeting a legitimate objective in a proportionate way, and making adjustments could end up costing your business money thereby making them unreasonable. In acknowledgement of the costs that are sometimes associated with making reasonable adjustments, the government has put into place the Access to Work (AtW) programme, which can provide grants to assist you in making those adjustments. An AtW grant might be used to make adjustments that make it possible for you to hire a disabled person with the skills you need or to retain an employee who develops a disability or long term condition (keeping their valuable skills and saving both time and money recruiting a replacement). Grants can be used to provide aids and equipment in the workplace, to assist with travel to work, to employ a support worker or a job coach.[6]

Dress codes

I often get asked by early years businesses to advise on issues that have arisen as a result of a member of staff wearing what the business owner considers to be inappropriate clothing, jewelry etc. Rightly the business owners are concerned about being labelled as discriminatory if the clothing is being worn for religious reasons. There have been a number of high profile cases reported in the press so this concern is not surprising.

As is so often the case, my first reaction is to ask the employer, 'What does it say in your dress code or uniform policy?' Settings that have a clear policy that sets out what is expected, what is inappropriate, giving clear non-discriminatory reasons for this (e.g., health and safety related reasons) are best placed to deal with these

6   The Access to Work Scheme can be found here: www.gov.uk/access-to-work/overview.

queries when they arise. But be careful not to simply disallow an item of dress just because you don't like it.

Shared Parental Leave

The last few years have seen a whole raft of employment law changes which have added layers of complexity for small businesses – pensions auto-enrolment, real time reporting and the right to request flexible working to mention just a few. But these almost pale into insignificance when compared with the complexities to be faced by small businesses as a result of the introduction of Shared Parental Leave. I don't intend to cover in detail the ins and outs of Statutory Maternity Pay but I will say a bit more about the new Shared Parental Leave arrangements.

The intention behind the legislation is to allow fathers to play a greater role in raising their child and to help mothers return to work when they want to without losing leave entitlement, or to return to work temporarily for a busy period. The rules also apply to same sex couples, and to couples adopting or involved in surrogacy.

Shared Parental Leave will allow parents to share statutory leave and pay following the birth of a child, by allowing mothers to choose to end their maternity leave at any point after the initial two week compulsory maternity leave period. The parents can then choose how to split the remaining 50 weeks of leave between them, taking leave either separately or at the same time.

The most challenging aspect of the legislation for small businesses is that parents may choose to take leave either as one continuous period or in discontinuous periods. This means that the mother can return to work for a while after the first two weeks, and then take another chunk of leave at a later date or dates. Similarly, the father can take Shared Parental Leave at any time within that 50 week period.

In order to manage Shared Parental Leave effectively you should read the eligibility criteria carefully and update your policies and procedures to reflect Shared Parental Leave. Your thinking when devising your policy should address how you plan to deal with requests for continuous blocks of leave (these requests cannot be refused), for example, making arrangements for maternity cover. Also consider how to respond to requests for discontinuous patterns of leave (these can be rejected on certain grounds but need to be managed objectively and with a view to avoiding any form of discrimination).[7]

Flexible working for all

On 30th June 2014 I celebrated the introduction of legislation giving every employee the right to request flexible working. This announcement meant a lot to me personally as it affirmed a view that I've held since I first became involved with the DTI Work-Life Balance Challenge Fund (WLB-CF) back in 2000. As part of the WLB-CF project, businesses were invited to apply for funds to help them to promote healthy work-life balance within their workforce. I enjoyed advising a number of businesses during the two years of the project who were beginning to recognise that if they could support their staff with managing their work-life balance this would bring benefits to the business as well as to the employees themselves. Those businesses began to acknowledge that work-life balance isn't just about mums, but applies to all of us. *Whether we are parents or not, we all have complex lives that we need to manage alongside our working lives.*

The years since then have added many additional challenges into the complexity of my own life and I am grateful that I've been able to work flexibly in order to manage that (although in the end I gave myself the ultimate flexibility by taking the decision to work for myself). So when the law changed I celebrated the fact that legislation now provides a requirement for every employee to have the right to request flexible working, and for their employers, at the very least, to consider that request in a reasonable manner (employers are not under any obligation to grant those requests) – regardless of their personal circumstances. I hope that you encourage productive dialogues with staff about how a healthy work-life balance can benefit both employees and the business.

If you want to find out more about applying work-life balance initiatives in your business, the evaluation report looking at the

---

7   Further information can be found at www.acas.org.uk/index.aspx?articleid=4911 and www.gov.uk/shared-parental-leave-and-pay-employer-guide

successes achieved as a result of the WLB-CF makes for interesting reading and is just as relevant to today's employers.[8]

Social media and digital communication

Social media and digital communication such as email, texting and instant messaging are a fundamental part of our personal and professional lives these days. And I can pretty much guarantee that almost every member of your staff makes regular and enthusiastic use of it. Digital communication brings great advantages, making it easy for us to connect and communicate with others, but also carries consequences when used by staff inappropriately.

Recent case law is increasingly highlighting examples of staff being disciplined or dismissed as a result of their inappropriate use of social media and other digital communication channels, and makes it clear that having a policy in place is the biggest single action that employers should take in this area to avoid unfortunate incidents. Having a social media and digital communication policy, communicating the policy with staff in a way that helps them to understand the consequences of actions they may take without thinking, and linking that policy to your disciplinary policy and any codes of conduct are essential steps for you to take.

These are some of the areas that are coming up regularly in case law, and in my own conversations with setting managers, and which should therefore be addressed within your policy:

- Use of equipment owned by the business for inappropriate personal activity, e.g., downloading porn, visiting prohibited sites using the setting's computers (this is a particular risk where staff are allowed to take work laptops home to complete planning activity and reports if the laptop is not password protected and may be used by other members of the staff member's household), sending inappropriate texts using a work mobile

- Doing personal business during working hours – a client recently dismissed a member of their administration staff

---

8   It can be found here www.tavinstitute.org/projects/report-the-evaluation-of-the-work-life-balance-challenge-fund.

after they reviewed the browsing history on her office PC and found that she was spending a good part of her day doing online shopping and visiting social media sites

- Data protection and confidentiality breaches – staff may deliberately misuse confidential information, but more often than not they do so through carelessness, e.g., by having personal data about children and their families on a laptop or memory stick that they take home, leave in their car, fail to password protect or encrypt, etc.

- Use of own devices, e.g. laptops, tablets and smartphones to undertake work-related activity – your policy should include a section on what is referred to as BYOD (Bring Your Own Device) setting out clearly:

  » How any work related information can be accessed and stored on those devices

  » How any confidential data should be protected using passwords or encryption

  » Your rights as an employer to access their device and the information it holds

- Inappropriate emails, posts, texts, etc. – unfortunately the behaviour of the playground sometimes follows people into the workplace; cyber-bullying (deliberate use of digital technology to upset someone) and harassment of colleagues can result in both the perpetrator and the employer being held liable through what is termed Vicarious Liability (as an employer you have a duty to protect your staff from any forms of bullying and harassment)

- Inappropriate use of mobile phones – this might include staff using their mobile phone in the setting, putting children at risk, use of work mobiles for personal calls, and making or receiving calls when driving

- Inappropriate posts on social media – even if the staff member tries to disassociate personal comments from work comments, e.g., by putting on their Twitter profile that 'all tweets reflect my personal views', inevitably if readers know that the person works in your setting, any views expressed may be read in that context. Such posts could risk bringing the setting into disrepute (which is likely to be treated as gross misconduct in your disciplinary policy). An employee whose privacy settings mean that a wide range of people can see their posts may decide to post negative comments about the setting such as moaning about their manager or about parents or children using the setting – this is fine when you're having a private chat with friends but not if that post is shared further afield.

Putting a policy in place is, of course, just a first step. Briefing and training staff is essential to ensure they are aware of your policy and understand what it means to them in terms of their day to day behaviour when using digital technology. So this should form part of your staff induction. Existing staff should also be asked to sign to say that they understand the policy. And, because technology is constantly evolving, your policy should be updated regularly to make sure it keeps pace with new ways of communicating.

If you decide that at some point you may wish to monitor a staff member's digital communications, for example their emails or their internet browsing history, do bear in mind that people have a right to privacy and may be upset by this. Monitoring is not in any way illegal but good practice would suggest that you inform staff in advance, by writing into your policy:

- that you may monitor their digital communication, stating which forms might be monitored

- what use you may make of that information, e.g., use CCTV footage as evidence of performance and behaviour

- who can access that information, e.g., the police, members of your committee, etc?

If you do use CCTV or other forms of recording, you should also alert visitors to your setting that CCTV is in use.[9]

---

9   Further information about this can be found at www.ico.org.uk.

People management challenges

The Chartered Management Institute (CMI) recently conducted a study on the management challenges facing managers in 2020 and beyond. The report entitled Management 2020, which can be accessed on the CMI website,[10] is the result of a major piece of research about the state of management and management skills in the UK and identifies the following areas as being priorities for the future:

- *Managing poor performance and low productivity* – unsurprisingly the report found that many managers lack the competence and confidence required to deal effectively with underperforming staff – this is by far the most common request for management training that I get from my clients across all sectors.

- *Managing inter-generational workforces* – with the removal of the default retirement age and the pushing back of the age when we can claim a state pension, your workforce may be made up of people from 17 to 70 years of age; managers need to understand and be able to deal with the very different needs and expectations of a workforce spanning four generations. In some cases existing business models will need to be adapted to accommodate those needs and expectations.

- *Low employee engagement* – particular concerns were identified around younger people (often referred to as 'Millennials' as they were born around the time of the new millennium) who seem to be coming into the workforce with different expectations about the purpose of work and work-life balance – managers in the early years sector repeatedly tell me how difficult they are finding it to engage these people in the work of the setting and the difficulties that their attitudes towards work present.

- *Lack of management training* – management is still seen as something that anyone can 'pick up' rather than a set of acquired skills. The CMI has now coined the phrase 'the accidental manager' which is how I've been describing

---

10   www.managers.org.uk/~/media/Files/PDF/M2020/Management%202020%20-%20Leadership%20to%20unlock%20long-term%20growth.pdf

early years business owners and managers for years. People who own and run early years businesses are often people who came into early years because it suited their lifestyle, or because they love working with children, and somehow have ended up owning and managing businesses with all the responsibilities that entails.

Having identified the problems, the CMI distilled the essence of good practice in management under three headings:

- *Purpose* – clarity and accountability

- *People* – preparing managers and leaders at all levels

- *Potential* – developing people to meet organisational needs of the future.

I'd like to give my slant on these areas as I see them in the early years and childcare sector.

Purpose – clarity and accountability

I can remember in years gone by working with the Investors in People Standard as an Adviser and supporting clients with a mantra of clarity of goals, clarity of roles and clarity of expectations. These formed the foundations of the Standard and were major factors that we typically found contributed to a sense of well-being for staff. Herzberg identified in his research back in 1959 that the true motivators that provide a sense of well-being are:

- *the work itself* – giving people a sense that what they do has purpose and meaning, and making the work itself interesting

- *responsibility* – giving someone a responsibility is the same as saying to them 'I trust you'; this is hugely motivating so make it clear what responsibilities you are entrusting to each staff member – let people own their role

- *achievement* – setting people up to succeed means making it clear what your expectations are; help them to understand 'what good looks like' and coach them in the steps they need to take to achieve this

- *recognition* – when people achieve and exceed your expectations make sure that you recognise their success in a way that is meaningful and appropriate to them (remember that this may not be the same way that would be meaningful for you)

- *advancement* – this might mean promoting someone, but can also mean giving them greater responsibility, encouraging them to learn, develop and grow – find out what advancement means to each member of your team.

People – preparing managers and leaders at all levels

Don't fall into the trap of employing a team of 'accidental managers'. Think carefully about the knowledge and skills that you need managers and team leaders in your setting to have in order to get the best from your staff and prepare a management development plan to ensure you support this. Your plan might include the steps you will take to recruit managers with the right competencies and/or to grow and develop your own. As a part of that plan don't forget about yourself – what skills and knowledge do you need to have in order to lead the business effectively?

Potential – developing people to meet organisational needs of the future

Think about the future not just about today. It's quite scary how rapidly the world of work is changing. One of the most significant challenges for educationalists is to develop a curriculum that will prepare the children and young people of today for jobs that we can't even begin to imagine yet. Today young people enter the workforce as web designers, virtual assistants, app developers, renewable energy engineers, Uber drivers to name just a few current career options.

And the world of an early years business is changing too. The PESTLE Analysis that we looked at back in Chapter 2 should have provided some insights into the ways in which your business model may need to change in the future. And your 7S Analysis should have helped you to think about how well equipped your staff will be to meet those changes. A business model designed to meet the changing needs of parents and the expectations of governments and of society will require a highly adaptive and flexible workforce supported by a team of strong and capable managers. There is more about supporting people through change later in Chapter 9.

The CMI have also developed a free Benchmarking Toolkit which you can access in order to benchmark management in your own business against the results from the research. [11]

It should be remembered that in settings run by Voluntary Management Committees, it is the trustees who employ the staff within the setting. They should recruit, manage and support senior managers and review their performance. They may also take part in the recruitment of other staff within the setting.

In my experience, breaches in employment law often occur when untrained committee members are expected to undertake key management functions such as conducting recruitment interviews, or disciplinary hearings.

So everything I have outlined above applies to them in the same way as it might apply to employed managers in settings. Considering the development needs of trustees is crucial as they are key participants in the management of staff within so many settings.

Key management skills

I'm going to cover a few of the people management issues for which managers in early years businesses most often seek my help.

Failing to delegate

One of the biggest complaints that staff make about their managers is lack of effective delegation. All too often managers either refuse to delegate, or delegate the wrong things, or delegate in such a way that people feel they've been set up to fail.

And this problem extends right at the very top in early years businesses with, for example, committee-run settings lacking clear arrangements in their constitution about what will be delegated to the management staff in the setting.

So here are a few tips to help you to think about delegation in your setting:

---

11   www.management2020.co.uk

- Thinking about why you should delegate can help you to select the right things to delegate and to delegate in an appropriate manner, giving the right messages to staff. Delegation is important to managers because it:

  » allows you to focus more of your time as a manager on things that can't be delegated and have to be done by you

  » enables you to provide development opportunities for staff

  » may help staff to feel more empowered – remember the earlier messages about 'I trust you'.

- There are times when you definitely shouldn't delegate, for example, because you don't like doing something or because you want to share or pass the blame, or because you just can't be bothered to do it yourself or think it is beneath you to do (changing nappies is often mentioned to me by early years staff).

- Recognise the things that can't be delegated – that must be done by you (perhaps for regulatory reasons).

- Delegate at the earliest opportunity, not once you've got half way through something (this can feel a bit like being offered a half-eaten toffee).

- Clarify the nature of the task and levels of responsibility you are delegating.

- Tell others what you have delegated and to whom – this confirms your confidence in them.

- Show faith in and support the person you have delegated to – believe they will do well and let them know this is how you feel.

- Agree the criteria to be used to decide if the task has been completed to the required standard and deadline.

- Give praise and recognition for work well done.

You might like to make use of this simple checklist when delegating a task to help you to cover all of these points in your conversation with your team member:

Question	You should cover:	Ask yourself:
What?	What are you delegating? Is it the whole of a task or just a part of it? Just this once or forever?	Have you been clear and specific?
Who?	Who have you decided to delegate this task to? How capable are they? How confident are they? Have they done it before? How much support or training will they need to enable them to do it?	Have you picked the person with the right level of skill, experience and confidence, considering the criticality of the task?
Why?	What is your reason for delegating this particular task to this person? Is it already part of their job or are you asking them to do something extra? What do you need to say to them to motivate them to take on this task and do it well?	Have you thought how you will justify your request to them?
How?	How much detail do you need to give them about how to perform the task? How will you get across to them the standard you require? How important is it that they do this in a certain way?	Have you made your expectations clear?
When?	What is your deadline? When do you expect them to do this? Do they have the time to do it? When and how will you review the completion of the task? Do you need to have interim milestones along the way to check on progress?	Are you being realistic about timescales?

Lack of team working

Many of my early years clients ask me to help them to improve the way their team of practitioners work together. To assist them with this I am frequently invited to deliver tailor-made team development days based on their specific needs and challenges.

More often than not the overall aim is to develop participants' understanding and appreciation of each other so that they can work towards becoming a more effective team. However, specific themes might include:

- improving communication

- developing partnerships with parents

- reducing conflict within the team

- helping staff to cope with change and work-related stress

- understanding what motivates team members

- building leadership and management capability.

I often incorporate a tool called the Jigsaw@work into these programmes as this is a practical tool that helps people to understand their own and other people's personality types and their preferred working styles. This understanding builds tolerance, respect and an appreciation of each other's strengths. Unlike typical psychometric profiling tools, the Jigsaw@work is simple and fun to use, with its tactile nature of appealing to the visual and kinaesthetic learning styles of many early years practitioners.

However, there is nothing to stop you from facilitating this sort of conversation yourself as part of a team meeting. You could access online tools to help you with this. But the most important thing is to open up an honest and supportive dialogue between your team members about how they each prefer to operate so that people begin to understand and therefore respect the differences between themselves and others.

Within this sort of meeting it's essential that you guide your team members to begin to express their appreciation of the natural abilities of their colleagues. Typical comments to encourage might include things like: 'We all know how well organised Joanne is, don't we', or, 'Tracy is just brilliant at coming up with new ideas for activities with the children'. Sew those seeds yourself and encourage others to contribute.

The next step is then to make sure that this dialogue continues on a day to day basis in the setting. One setting in Cambridge made this work for them following the team development event I ran for them. The setting had a team of very skilful practitioners; however, the manager felt that they didn't know how to work as a team very well. Following a team meeting where I helped them to begin to build their understanding of each other's working styles, they created a team wall display for their staff room; next to each staff member's photo they had added the key characteristics (both the positives and the challenges) for that person's style. There was a blank sheet of paper as a part of the display where team members were invited to make suggestions about how they could work together more effectively as a team. Last time I visited there was a suggestion for a team evening out to help a new team member to get to know everyone informally. This valuable and very visible reminder ensured that the team continued that positive dialogue on a day to day basis.

When driving performance becomes bullying

When we talk about bullying in the workplace it's easy to assume that all bullying is intentional; the behaviour of nasty people with some sort of axe to grind. But this isn't always the case. Some time ago, in the course of supporting a government department to deliver 360 degree feedback for their middle managers, I came across a man called Jeff. Jeff had been employed by the department for most of his working life and had risen up through the ranks through internal promotion. At the time of receiving his 360 degree feedback report he was in his early 50s and operating as a regional manager with six managers reporting into him.

In his self-assessment Jeff described himself as having very strong leadership qualities and being able to inspire and motivate others. He described himself as 'a great motivator' whose team was successful, regularly exceeding targets. Whilst feedback from his line manager agreed with Jeff's self assessment, feedback from his team variously described him in less positive ways including:

'He's a bully'

'He constantly harasses staff about targets'

'I've had to take time off sick with stress because of the way he speaks to me'.

When I sat down with Jeff to go through his report with him, he was clearly shocked and quite distressed. He couldn't understand why, in more than 20 years of management, no one had ever given him this sort of feedback before. He truly believed that the behaviour described by others as bullying was him being strong, motivational and inspiring. When I explored Jeff's situation in more detail, it turned out that he'd never received any training on how to motivate his staff (it was assumed that because his team was successful he was doing a good job) and he had never asked for feedback from the people who really mattered – his staff.

Attracting and retaining quality staff in low paid jobs

Having a good understanding of what motivates people to come and work for your setting is important. Have you asked your recently appointed staff why they wanted to join you? And what makes your more experienced staff want to stay?

Some research that I conducted with a day nursery found that although people are concerned about pay and other financial rewards, they agreed that there are many other things that help them feel motivated. They told me that they felt valued when they were recognised and rewarded in the following ways:

- training and development:

  » staff were allowed to attend external training and skills development

  » study leave/paid time off was available for professional development

  » exam/professional/supervision fees were paid for

- support to do the job:

  » team building events helped staff get to know their colleagues better in a less formal situation

  » management listened to staff feedback and ensured timely and appropriate support was provided when staff were having problems

- work-life balance:

  » staff could chose to take extra paid holiday instead of other rewards for excellent performance

- » flexibility was allowed to help staff to manage their personal lives

- appreciation:
  - » staff liked being thanked by management
  - » they felt appreciated by being given extra/different responsibilities, or being promoted
  - » there was public acknowledgement of achievements at team meetings, or in newsletters
  - » awards, e.g., employee of the month/year made staff feel special
  - » gift vouchers or other small tokens of appreciation were given to say thank you.

Many of these have little cost. What is essential is to reward performance in ways that are relevant and meaningful to each individual. What works for one person in your team may not work for another. So having a conversation with each staff member about this as a part of your appraisal discussion is helpful.

Training staff on a limited budget

One of the outcomes of an appraisal should be an agreed training and development plan for each individual. In most businesses, the desire for training and development far outstrips any budget that might be available to pay for courses and qualifications. It is therefore essential that managers think and act responsibly in relation to people's development needs. The training and development plan should not be a 'wish list' of courses that people fancy attending.

The following series of questions (which should be addressed in this order) will help you to establish priorities effectively:

1. What is required by statute/regulations?

2. What is essential to enable the person to do their current job effectively?

3. What could help the person to do their job even more effectively in the future?

4. What could prepare the person for a future role that we might need them to take on?

5. What would motivate the person to become more committed/ motivated?

In reality we seldom have the luxury of money left over to cover priority number five, so the trick is making sure that, once priorities have been established, you think creatively about the most cost effective solutions to meeting people's needs. The instinct in many settings in the past was simply to pass staff a copy of their local authority training catalogue and let them take their pick. This was an ok (but not ideal) thing to do in the past when such training was provided on a fully subsidised basis by the local authorities. Now that this is not the case, more commercial consideration needs to be given to this process in order to make best use of staff time and budgets.

Developing staff is not just about sending people on a course; it includes any activity which develops knowledge, skills or attitude. The majority of this is likely to take place in the workplace. Here are some suggestions, some of which you may not have considered previously and may be unfamiliar with (so I will provide a brief explanation of each):

- *Internal talks* – Identify those members of your team who excel in various aspects of the role and get them to give a talk to the rest of the team or run a short training session in a team meeting.

- *Coaching* – Develop the coaching skills of line managers and room leaders so that they can support the development of team members effectively on the job.

- *External courses* – If the skills you need staff to develop are generic (i.e. not early years specific) don't just rely on courses provided by the local authority and early years agencies to provide these, look at other providers of training such as your local Enterprise Agency, Chamber of Commerce or Voluntary Sector Training organisation as well as private training providers.

- *Secondments* – A secondment involves a member of your team going to work elsewhere for a period of time in order to develop best practice approaches that can be brought back into your setting. This could involve something as minor as a secondment to another room within your setting, or a move to another setting within your chain if you run more than one nursery, or even an external secondment such as time working on a project for the Pre-school Learning Alliance (PLA) or National Day Nurseries Association (NDNA).

- *Personal study/research projects* – Ask a staff member to research best practice in a particular topic or approach (this may tie in with work they are doing to complete an early years qualification). You could follow this up by asking them to develop a new approach, process or methodology to be introduced into your setting.

- *Mentoring* – Develop the mentoring skills of your senior team to enable them to support and advise their colleagues in a way which will be well-received as a positive and supportive intervention.

- *Benchmarking* – Compare how other organisations and do something in order to develop your own practice. Benchmarking works best if it is not with an immediate competitor (this encourages openness and honesty) and if it is two way (I'll show you mine if you show me yours). It can sometimes be worth benchmarking with businesses from outside of the sector if you'd like to develop a process in your setting that is generic, e.g. marketing or handling complaints.

- *Shadowing* – Identify members of your team who do things really well and ask other members of staff to watch them and identify how they could adapt/improve their own practice.

- *Team meetings* – Include an aspect of development or practice improvement at each of your team meetings to ensure they have a positive focus.

- *Feedback* – Bill Gates, the Founder of Microsoft, is often quoted as saying, 'We all need people who will give us feedback – that's how we improve'. But feedback skills are often lacking in early years businesses so that when feedback is given to staff it comes across negatively, is not well received and can be damaging to relationships. Developing the feedback skills of your senior team is essential. Without constructive feedback staff may not be aware of the areas where they need to improve and develop.

- *Conferences and exhibitions* – The providers of early years conferences and exhibitions are increasingly running these at locations around the country making them more accessible. If you or a member of your team attends a conference or exhibition as a development activity it's important to plan in advance what you wish to find out about because it's easy at this sort of event to become distracted. So research beforehand who the speakers and exhibitors will be and plan your day.

- *Job swaps* – This involves two members of your team swapping jobs for a period of time to learn how the other team operates.

- *Visits to other settings* – At many of the workshops that I deliver, setting owners and managers exchange contact details and arrange to go and visit each other's settings. The feedback I have received about these visits has been extremely positive.

- *Team events* – I often work with settings to facilitate team building events focused on improving staff commitment and communication. On other occasions I work with members of the senior team to help them to design a team event that they then deliver themselves.

- *Qualifications* – Of course there are mandatory qualifications that various members of your team might complete, but you may also want to consider encouraging them to complete additional qualifications as this both enhances their knowledge and skills whilst at the same time providing them with a recognised qualification. Consideration about the payment for this may be an issue (see below).

- *Social media* – This should be considered a valuable element of CPD. Staff can benefit by following/connecting with people and organisations who post useful information relevant to early years providers. They can also join relevant groups in LinkedIn or take part in relevant Twitter Hours such as #EYTalking where early years related topics are discussed within a facilitated discussion. And of course use of social media is free.

Over recent years early years businesses have been faced with increasing costs associated with staff training as local authorities have been forced to move to a more commercial Traded Service environment where settings are expected to pay for training. This situation will increase over coming years as the requirement for local authorities to pass onto settings more of the funding they receive for early years provision means that they will face further reductions in the services that they can provide to settings at a fully or partially subsidised rate.

In addition to the withdrawal of subsidised training by local authorities, changes to the funding of apprenticeships introduced in 2017 will require a cash contribution from early years providers and a specified amount of time spent by the apprentice on off the job training. The advent of both of these changes at the same time, mean a big change in the way that early years providers need to plan for and budget for staff training.

It has come as a shock to many early years businesses that they now need to budget for training in the same way as small businesses in other sectors have to. This shift also means that the local authority may not be the best provider of training services so starting to shop around has been a new experience for some. Many are finding that they can contract directly with the external training providers who previously offered services through the local authority at a more competitive rate. The new apprenticeship arrangements are specifically designed to encourage employers to shop around and to negotiate the best deal. But it does mean taking the time to shop around and to negotiate with providers in a way that was not required before.

One organisation that can help with your search for well qualified, professional training providers is the National Early Years Trainers & Consultants Organisation (NEyTCO). They have built an extensive database of members who offer a wide range of training and consultancy services to the sector. They also provide the following guidelines on choosing an appropriate training provider or consultant to meet your needs:

- *Clear requirements*

  » Be clear about what you are looking for – what are you trying to achieve?

  » How does their expertise match your requirements?

  » Consider making the training cost effective by splitting the cost with another provider

  » Be clear about costs – are other expenses, such as accommodation or travel, included?

- *Professional qualifications*

  » Check they are registered with a professional association by asking them for their membership number

  » What qualifications do they have that you can use to reassure yourself they have demonstrated an appropriate level of understanding of their subject?

  » Don't be afraid to ask them how they maintain and enhance their own Continuous Personal Development

  » Do they have a formal qualification to teach adults, such as PTLLS (Preparation for Teaching in the Lifelong Learning Sector) or Certificate in Education (training in teaching at further or higher education level)?

- *Checks*

  » Check their identity

  » It is vital that they have insurance, for example: Employers Liability, professional indemnity and public/product liability

  » What do other providers say about the consultant or trainer?

  » Can they supply two references and/or testimonials to support their work?

» Do they supply delegate evaluations?

- *The products on offer*

  » Do they offer a range of services that might be of use to you?

  » Can you refine their 'standard' offering to fit your setting and your requirements?

  » How do they support reflective practice?

  » Will the cost include documents, certificate of attendance or any reports?

  » Clarify the terms and conditions. (Source: NEyTCO Choosing a Consultant.)

Changes to the way in which the government funds apprenticeship programmes are also creating challenges for early years businesses. At the time of writing, the practical arrangements are soon to be implemented and the challenges are still being debated. So I can't comment further on the outcome of this. Whatever the outcome, what is certain is that early years businesses will be expected to bear more of the costs associated with staff training in the future. Because of this, many early years business owners are concerned about staff leaving once they have completed a qualification, leaving the setting out of pocket after they have invested heavily in that member of staff. If you do decide to support a staff member with a non-statutory training programme you could consider asking them to make a contribution to the costs.

Another option to consider is the introduction of a training agreement that allows the business to recover the costs of training from a staff member who leaves during or shortly after completing a training programme or qualification. In order to do this legally, a written training agreement should be put in place before the training programme starts. This should set out clearly what percentage of the cost would be reclaimed (a sliding scale is useful) depending on when they leave. Typically this might stipulate 100 per cent to be clawed back if they leave within three months of the end of the programme, 75 per cent within 3–6 months, 50 per cent within 6–9 months, with no repayment after 12 months.

It is important to make it clear in the agreement what the method of repayment will be, for example a deduction from their wages, and the staff member should be asked to sign to accept the agreement.

Finally, a word about the importance of evaluating the effectiveness of any training and development that you provide for your staff. You might consider doing this as a part of the appraisal review by answering the following questions in discussion with each team member:

- What development activity have you taken part in since your last review?

- What have you learnt?

- What can you do now/do better that you couldn't do before?

- What difference has it made to your performance?

- How has this impacted on the children, parents, colleagues, and the business as a whole?

- Has this development need been met in full?

- Has this learning highlighted any other development that needs to take place?

Dealing with pensions and retirement issues

The government's plans for auto-enrolment are now well advanced with, at the time of writing this book, all but the very smallest of businesses already engaged in the process. There are still those who haven't reached their staging date yet and for those my advice is to heed the warnings made by some of the businesses who engaged with this process earlier. Employers who have been through the process warn against making *any* of the following assumptions:

- 'Our payroll provider or pension provider will sort it all out for us.' – It will be down to you to make suitable arrangements for your business and you will need to collate the relevant information yourself.

- 'We've already got a pension scheme in place so we won't have to do anything.' – Your existing pension arrangements may not be compliant with the auto-enrolment criteria so check with your pension provider at the earliest opportunity.

- 'It's like the stakeholder pensions – we're excluded because we employ fewer than 5 people.' – Businesses that employ only one person (the owner of the business) are the only ones that are excluded.

- 'Most of my staff will opt out.' – This was a very common assumption in the early days but experience has shown that fewer than 15% of those eligible have opted out rather than the 28% the Department for Work and Pensions originally estimated.[12]

- 'Surely we won't have to do it if it puts us out of business.' – When I began having discussions with early years business owners there was a big assumption that if they couldn't afford to make the required contributions to their staff pensions, they would be somehow let off – this is of course not the case, so building pension contributions into your financial forecasts is essential.

The Pensions Regulator provides excellent information for employers about the process of auto-enrolment on their website.[13]

Retirement has generally become more challenging to manage over recent years, not just because of the costs associated with auto-enrolment, but also since the removal of the default retirement age. In the past if you had an older employee who was not performing as well as you would wish, you could quite easily apply your default retirement age and ask them to retire. This is now very hard to justify. The only real option now is to use your performance management arrangements and focus on their lack of capability as valid grounds for dismissal.

It is good practice to ask open questions regarding an employee's plans for the future as part of your formal appraisal process but you should avoid asking any direct questions such as 'Are you planning to retire in the near future?' as this would be considered discriminatory.

---

12 See www.behaviouralinsights.co.uk
13 www.thepensionsregulator.gov.uk/employers/getting-ready-for-automatic-enrolment.aspx

ACAS has published guidance for employers on employing older workers[14] and has also recently produced a research report on this topic.[15]

Varying contracts of employment

It's not unreasonable to expect that at some point, a contract of employment might need to be changed, for example, changing working hours in response to the delivery of extended hours for parents or where an employee has submitted a request to work flexibly.

An existing contract of employment can be varied, but only with the agreement of both parties. It is, after all, a contract agreed by both parties. If you do wish to make changes to existing contracts, here are a few tips:

- Check what your existing contract allows you to vary without consultation (a well-drafted contract should allow you some flexibility to make certain variations as the demands of the business change) and provide a month's notice in writing of any changes already allowed by your contract.

- Discuss other proposed changes with employees and negotiate to gain their agreement – you may need to be prepared to compromise, to offer an incentive to accept the changes and to consider staff who would be disadvantaged by the changes you are proposing (especially if that disadvantage could be considered discriminatory).

- Changes can be agreed either on an individual basis with your staff or through a collective agreement if you have staff affiliated to a trade union or other representative body.

- Give a month's notification of the changes in writing.

- Consider building greater flexibility into contracts for future employees, making it easier to make future changes (getting this right can be tricky so appropriate advice should be sought if you plan to do this).

---

14   www.acas.org.uk/index.aspx?articleid=3203
15   www.acas.org.uk/media/pdf/f/i/Managing-older-workers-a-report-for-acas.pdf

If you can't reach agreement with your staff, and decide that your business would suffer as a result of not making changes, your only option would be to terminate the existing contract dismissing the employee(s) and asking people to reapply for jobs with the revised contract. This should be treated as a last resort and would, of course, require you to follow a fair dismissal process and offer the employee the right of appeal against their dismissal. It may also result in having to pass Statutory Redundancy Pay.

Chapter 7

RUNNING AN EARLY YEARS BUSINESS ON A DAY TO DAY BASIS

I can't emphasise enough the importance of early years businesses becoming more self-sufficient in terms of business practice due to the reduction in business support from local authorities. This will mean building your own capability, and also creating a support network for yourself of advisers and sources of information for high quality, up to date business advice.

As your early years provision grows, inevitably so do your business and administrative tasks. Your original aim when you started your early years business may have been to work with children and suddenly you find yourself stuck with endless paperwork and dealing with a mountain of bureaucracy. Being able to keep your finger on the pulse of your business in a quick and easy manner will ensure you are better placed to make decisions about the future of your business by having the right information at the right time, and to do so in a time efficient manner.

In this chapter I am going to help you to think about how to do this on a day to day basis to help to keep your early years business operating efficiently, effectively and in a legal and compliant manner. This will help to inform the business effectiveness part of your Early Years Business Dashboard.

Data protection registration

I have had many discussions with early years settings over the years about whether they need to register under the Data Protection Act or not. Arguments I've been given for not registering have included things like 'we only hold paper records – nothing is held on computer' and 'we only hold the information that parents have given to us' and 'we're only small'. The 1998 Act sets out the regulatory framework which needs to be complied with by any organisation that holds what is classed as personal data – regardless of the format that the information is held in and regardless of how that information has been obtained. Personal data might typically include names, addresses, and contact details, and other personal information about staff, parents and children so that's why early years businesses are included in the registration requirement.

The regulations require businesses to register with the Information Commissioners Office on an annual basis. This is a very straightforward process and costs £35.00 a year (don't be tempted by offers by organisations to complete the registration process for you for a price that is higher than this – it is a well-known scam). What I will say about the registration process is to make sure you understand the language being used (for example, it uses the phrase 'The Data Controller' to mean the person in your business who has responsibility for making sure that any personal data you hold is looked after properly). The form also asks you to tick which types of data you hold, so think carefully and if you're not sure if you do or if you might in the future, just tick the box in case – there is no extra cost for ticking more categories.

Once you have registered you will be given a registration number and will receive a reminder every year which asks you simply to confirm if things are still the same and to re-register. So that's all very straightforward.

The more challenging aspect of data protection is then to make sure that the way in which you deal with personal data is in compliance with good practice. Asking yourself the following questions will help you to do this:

- Do you really need this information about an individual? Do you know what you're going to use it for? Collecting information is fine but if that is all you do, it will have been a pointless exercise. It is sometimes tempting to collect information just because it is easily available. But if it is not of genuine use to your business, don't bother.

- Do the people whose information you hold know that you've got it, and are they likely to understand what it will be used for? If not you should inform them.

- If you need to pass on information (e.g., sharing information about a child with the primary school they are moving to or with the police if a child is considered to be at risk), would the people whose information you hold expect you to do this? If not explain your policy on sharing information – who will you share information with and in what circumstances.

- How do you ensure the information is being held securely, whether it's on paper or on computer? Put in place policies and procedures and train your staff on this.

- Is access to personal information limited to those who absolutely need to know? Password-protect computer files that contain personal data and keep paper records in a locked cupboard or drawer.

- How do you make sure the personal information is accurate and up to date? Ask the person involved to confirm the accuracy of the information you hold and to update it annually.

- Do you delete or destroy personal information as soon as you have no more need for it? In some cases you may need to keep data for some years to comply with regulations, but if you don't, then have a procedure for regularly weeding unnecessary information out and destroying it securely.

- Have you trained your staff in their responsibilities under the Data Protection Act? How do you check that they are fulfilling them in practice? Regular updates are important as are regular audits.

Managing information efficiently

Information starts out life just as data – a list of bills paid, invoices issued, staff time sheets, registers of attendance, etc. If your data is not well maintained, you are likely to have difficulty collecting what you need and your information is likely to be flawed. This could lead you to make inaccurate assumptions or inappropriate decisions about your business.

Gathering data

The way in which you collect data needs to be extremely efficient, and should fit in as a natural part of people's day to day activity. If it is not, the likelihood is that people will forget or be too busy to do it without considerable nagging. Consider how the data you need to run your business could be collected most efficiently. Also ask yourself how frequently each sort of data needs to be collected and reported on – some will be daily, some weekly, some monthly and some less frequently, say once a quarter or even just once a year.

Turning data into meaningful information

Once your data has been gathered, the next step is to put it into a format that makes it useful from a business point of view. Useful management information (or MI, as it is often referred to) will highlight differences between what you forecast and what is actually happening, showing you patterns, trends and anomalies. This will help you to predict and anticipate potential problems, and take timely corrective action before problems become too serious. Looking forward, good MI will ensure that you make well informed decisions about the future of your business and that you are able to prevent problems from occurring. This should be included in the current section of the Early Years Business Dashboard.

You can, of course, manage an early years business purely on paper, and indeed when I first started working in the sector this was quite common. However, increasingly, with various government organisations such as HMRC and local authorities expecting us to deal with them digitally, almost all providers, even the very smallest, have embraced IT and turned to digital solutions to do more and more. Here are some of the pros and cons of various options that you might consider for managing MI.

Paper-based systems	
Advantages:	Disadvantages:
• Costs nothing except your time • Completely tailored to your business	• Extremely time consuming to maintain and update • Difficult to scenario plan • Relies on good maths so subject to human error • No backup – if it gets lost or destroyed, it's gone
Digital systems that you create yourself (e.g. Excel or Access database)	
Advantages:	Disadvantages:
• Inexpensive software • Most PCs already have Excel installed as part of MS Office • Widely available free online help and advice • Access to low cost training through LearnDirect • Compatible with most other applications • Completely tailored to your business • Can be adapted as you go on to meet the different requirements of your business	• It's down to you to create something to fit an early years business • Design requires internal expertise or external consultancy support to create formulas • Need to design your own templates • Lack of support if it goes wrong • Have to do the updates yourself
Nursery management software	
Advantages:	Disadvantages:
• Especially designed for early years • Design work is done for you • Support and training usually offered as part of the deal • Technical helpline provided • Provides professional templates for forms, invoices etc.	• Relatively costly to purchase • Have to undergo training • Limited ability to tailor to your business (or costly to do so) • Once you've committed to a system it's complicated to move to a different one

Choosing and using specialist software

There are a number of software providers who offer specialist nursery management software packages and, while I'm not in a position to recommend a specific one for your early years business, I am grateful to Luke Francis from nursery software company, Parenta, for sharing the following checklist to help you to think through the various factors involved in choosing a suitable software provider for your setting.

- *Functionality* – It has to be fit for purpose. All early years businesses have different processes and calculate fees in different ways, so make sure it is flexible enough to accommodate the way you work. Make sure you are shown how your most complex child/account would work on the system.

- *Security* – Check how and where the data is held. Make sure that it is backed up, ideally automatically by the software provider, or sometimes it can be your responsibility to remember to do this.

- *Support and training* – You can have the most fantastic system but if you and your staff can't use it then there is no point in buying it. Check if training is included in the set up costs and if follow up training for new staff is also provided. Detailed user manuals and online help are also helpful.

- *Costs* – Make sure there are no nasty hidden costs. Some providers will charge extra for things like training, upgrades or additional users. Ask for all costs involved and check whether they have fee increases, whether they have any planned or when the last one was. Take care if you want them to tailor parts of the system to meet your needs – that can get very expensive.

- *Return on investment* – Software can be expensive short term but usually becomes cost effective when you think how it saves your time, parent relationships, costs of stationery, and even your reputation. Make sure it is actually going to save you time. It could be the deciding factor for a parent when looking at you and your competitors, more so now than ever.

- *Contract* – Do not get tied into a lengthy contract, always ask the cancellation policy.

- *Requirements* – Confirm what computer hardware you need to be able to use the software. Ask them to demonstrate that it will work with the equipment that you already have.

- *The provider* – Check out that the provider is reputable. How long they have been around and whether lots of other providers use them are good indicators. It can't hurt to do a credit check on the company, after all you are investing into them. Ask for references from other providers and Google them to see what people might be saying about them online.

Management reporting

You will need to have some sort of system to report on management information in a way that is digestible to the intended audience. This might include, for example, reporting to committee members or trustees who are volunteers and have limited time to get to grips with information prior to a meeting. The way you report information also needs to enhance your ability to make well-informed decisions about your business. So you then need to think about what you need to report on and the format it needs to be in to be of most value to you. Here are a few tips:

- Start by thinking about who the report will go to. What will their needs be?

- Consider the time constraints of the recipients and then try to produce simple, single page reports (dashboards) that summarise key information.

- Remember that graphs and diagrams, rather than spreadsheets of numbers, are often easier to digest and understand.

- And make sure you add some notes as a narrative or an executive summary to explain what they are looking at, and key issues or concerns raised in the report.

Policies and procedures

As an early years business you need to make sure that you have appropriate policies and procedures in place. Just to clarify the language I am using:

- A policy sets out your expectations and intentions and makes a commitment to them.

- A procedure sets out your detailed approach; how the policy should be implemented on a day to day basis; it may include a defined process.

Policies and procedures are useful because they can be used to train and provide guidance to staff and they make your expectations clear to everyone who comes into contact with the setting, including staff, parents, visitors and, of course, the children, providing a legal and ethical framework for everyone connected with the setting.

Policies and procedures are often overlooked and are acknowledged as being most valuable in situations where a dispute or disagreement has arisen. I have so many conversations with business owners seeking advice about a problem and my first question to them is usually 'What does your policy/procedure say?' Their relief is palpable when they describe a well drafted policy and I am able to say, 'Well, just do that then'. Often I have helped or advised them to put those policies into place and they thank me for doing so, even if they didn't really appreciate it at the time.

But it is worth stressing that you should never assume you don't need policies and procedures because:

- everyone thinks the same way as you do (they probably don't)

- you can create a policy at a later date if ever the need arises (you may not be allowed to create one retrospectively)

- you will never be challenged legally (we live in an increasingly litigious society so you may well be challenged)

- if you are challenged you'll be able to come to some sort of agreement (once people have commenced a legal process, reaching agreement is likely to be an expensive option).

Policies and procedures are often a requirement; this may include those that are a legal requirement, for example, a health and safety policy; those that are a regulatory requirement, for example, a safeguarding policy; those that are a contractual requirement, for example, some local authorities expect settings to have a fees policy and those that are simply recognised good practice, for example, a digital communication and social media policy.

Staff related policies and procedures

NCVO provides the following list of essential staff-related policies (NCVO members can access examples of these for free from their website):

- Recruitment and selection procedure (including DBS checks and other safer recruitment arrangements)

- Equal opportunities policy

- Dignity at work policy (including harassment and bullying)

- Discipline and grievance procedures

- Health and safety policy (where five or more staff are employed)

- Code of conduct (behavioural 'rules' specific to your business)

- Sickness absence procedure (including pay rates, reporting arrangements, absence monitoring)

- Annual leave procedure (including public holidays, carrying forward leave, requesting holiday, pro rata entitlement for part-time staff)

- Procedure regarding other types of absence including unauthorised absence, compassionate leave, career breaks and other leave e.g. jury service, time off for public duties etc.

- Family related policies (including parental leave and pay)

- Retirement policy

- Right to request flexible working procedure

- Pay procedure (including the treatment of deductions from pay e.g. pensions).

Some of the above will be covered by the statement of employment particulars (i.e. contract of employment), which is also an essential document.

Other policies and procedures

Other 'good to have' policies and procedures could include:

- Policies and procedures for volunteers including committee members

- Financial procedures

- Complaints procedure

- Performance management procedure

- Training policy

- Whistle-blowing procedure

- Diversity policy

- Digital communications policy

- Data protection/confidentiality policy

- Expenses policy

- Risk management procedures.

Polices relating to the children in your care

As an early years business there are also regulatory requirements set out in the EYFS for policies in relations to the safeguarding of children in your care such as:

- Fire safety procedure

- Accident and incident Emergency closure policy

- Behaviour management policy

- Disposal of nappies, aprons and gloves procedure

- Inclusion policy including SEND

- Intimate Care Policy

- Key person policy

- Lost or missing child policy

- Medication policy

- Nappy changing policy

- Operational procedures for outings

- Risk assessment and risk-benefit analysis

- Settling in policy

- Safeguarding children and child protection policy (including whistleblowing).

Polices relating to parents

Having a series of good policies in place that form a part of your contract with parents will help to protect your early years business in situations where a dispute or disagreement with a parent may arise. Good policies to have in place include:

- Admissions policy

- Non-attendance policy

- Non-collection of child policy

- Payment of fees policy (including non-payment, late payment, etc.)

- Complaints policy.

Keeping your policies and procedures up to date

Often early years businesses get themselves into trouble with the authorities because they have inadvertently overlooked legal requirements or the fact that legal requirements have changed. Keeping up to date with the plethora of laws, rules and regulations that affect small businesses is tough in any sector, but is perhaps especially tough in our sector as we have the added layer of Ofsted to comply with and this very often looms larger in our minds than other regulations. We can be in danger of overlooking other bodies, such as the Health and Safety Executive which regulate certain aspects of our businesses.

First of all, you should make sure that you take a systematic approach to reviewing policies and procedures in order to ensure they are up to date and also that they are fit for purpose as your early years business changes. You can either blitz the lot at one single point in the year or have a rolling programme of policies to be reviewed at certain dates throughout each year. This can often make more sense, as changes to legal requirements and other regulations don't tend to take place at the same time. You should also systematically review policies and procedures whenever you make a significant change in your business such as changing the age range or your opening hours, or making changes to your premises.

You should make sure that as policies and procedures are updated that proper version control is used so that staff can immediately locate the most recent version, and that they are put into practice effectively within the setting through communication with staff.

Make sure that you have an efficient method of receiving notification when legal and regulatory requirements change where someone else has done the hard work of trawling through the rules and regulations so that you don't have to (unless you really need to understand the details). This might include:

- Following government departments and other reputable organisations on Twitter – most of them tweet important news and changes with links to the relevant sections on their websites which I find provides a very quick headline of things that I can then bookmark to read in more detail later along with a link to the relevant documentation online so I don't have to search for it myself (you'll find lists of useful Twitter accounts to follow in the bibliography section at the end of the book, with a longer list available by visiting my Twitter profile @jacquiburkefp and going to my Lists)

- Signing up for update emails from those trusted and reliable organisations – most, such as HMRC and ACAS, allow you to tailor your areas of interest so that you only receive news about the things that are of interest to you (you'll find a list of useful links in the bibliography section at the end of the book)

- Attending an annual employment law update (ACAS run a programme of regular events around the country as do other organisations)

- Making sure that, if you outsource any of your functions, such as HR or financial management, your provider offers an update service

- Making full use of legal helplines – we often have these included as a part of our membership of various organisations or as a part of various insurance policies that we hold; 'If in doubt, give them a shout' is one of my mottos.

Check before you act

I can't tell you how many conversations I have with businesses about people management problems in particular that make my hair stand on end! These conversations usually start with something like 'We've got this member of staff we're having a bit of a problem with…'. The conversation then often reveals that a long-standing problem hasn't been addressed; it's festered and become a major issue. Management have got to the end of their tether and have now taken action. It then emerges that they've taken action prompted by their frustration and without taking the trouble to check any changes in the law or to fully consider the consequences of those actions. So a couple of thoughts:

- Don't take action when you're feeling angry, desperate or frustrated – pause, take a deep breath and think carefully first.

- Take time to refer to the latest version of your policies and procedures before acting and check when these were most recently updated.

- If you are in any doubt that you may not be approaching things in the right way, or you think that your policies may be out of date, check by making contact with the helpline of the relevant organisation.

In the case of employment law issues, unless you have a legal service available to you through one of your membership organisations, check with ACAS. I keep the ACAS Helpline number permanently pinned to my notice board as a constant reminder that if I'm in doubt I should give them a shout. They are really helpful people, will speak with you anonymously and will signpost you to further information on their website if you need it.

The time management challenge

With all of this to consider and keep on top of, is it any wonder that you end up feeling that there aren't enough hours in the day to get everything done? Many of the early years owners and managers that I work with report regularly working excessive hours and taking paperwork home with them, causing disruption and stress to their personal lives and ultimately damaging their physical and mental health.

Developing good personal time management habits and personal effectiveness by applying a few simple techniques to your work and personal life is essential to avoid overload and burn-out. Use the following techniques to help you to take some steps to manage your time and improve your work-life balance.

Step 1: First of all assess your time management habits and behaviour. You may find you are your own worst enemy. Identify which of your time management habits you need to change.

	Time management behaviour	Rating scale 0 = Never 1 = Rarely 2 = Occasionally 3 = Usually 4 = Always
1	I develop a fixed daily routine and do certain things at certain times.	
2	I put off things if they are not important.	
3	I do things adequately well and avoid seeking perfection.	
4	I finish a task before beginning another one.	
5	I group similar tasks together and do them together, e.g. financial tasks, phone calls.	
6	I think before I act.	
7	I decide what I must achieve at the beginning of each day.	
8	I begin my day with the most important things that I need to achieve.	
9	I avoid interrupting/distracting myself.	
10	I schedule regular thinking, planning and preparation time.	
11	I prepare so that everything I need to complete a task is there before I begin it.	
12	I understand the times of day when I am at my best.	
13	I allocate my most difficult and important tasks to my best times of the day.	

	Time management behaviour	Rating scale 0 = Never 1 = Rarely 2 = Occasionally 3 = Usually 4 = Always
14	I complete my work within normal working hours and avoid taking work home.	
15	I collect all my ideas together in one place, e.g. in a notebook.	
16	I do one thing at a time.	
17	I set myself time limits for tasks and stick to them.	
18	I rest before I become exhausted.	
19	I avoid doing jobs that should be done by someone else.	
20	I delegate aspects of my job to others in my team.	

Step 2: Next, identify what I call your time bandits (the things that seem to gobble up your valuable time leaving you feeling that you've been busy all day but not really achieved anything). Consider ways that you could minimise the negative impact that they have on your working day.

Step 3: Keep a time log for a couple of days and then reflect on how you are spending your time. Most of us find that much of what we spend time on doesn't directly contribute towards our business results. Can you identify the things you do that really make a difference? Using different coloured highlighters categorise each block of your activity as follows:

- I was doing the right task at the right time

- I was doing the right task, but at the wrong time

- I could have delegated this task to someone else

- This task was a complete waste of time – why was I doing it at all?

Step 4: Our tendency is often to pick things up, get interrupted or lose our train of thought, put them down again, start them again, put them down again several times. We can find that we return to a task several times during the course of the day, each time handling the same task again and feeling that we're starting from scratch again because the interruption has broken our concentration. This wastes effort and energy. Applying the 3Ds can help you to waste less effort and energy by ensuring that you touch each task only once. The 3Ds are:

- *Do it!* Look at it as a series of small tasks rather than one big one and complete at least the first part of the task straight away.

- *Delegate it!* Identify a task that uses more of your time than can be justified by the results and identify a person in your team who has, or could develop, the skills to take it on.

- *Dump it!* Get into the habit of opening your post with the bin in front of you. Don't be tempted to open emails that are clearly spam or are simply not of interest to you – delete them without opening so you don't get distracted by them. If it is not directly relevant to your business objectives, dump it straight away.

Step 5: Prioritise tasks using an Urgent/Important Matrix; this will help you to keep focused on completing your important tasks before they become urgent. If you spend all your time doing things that are both urgent and important you are likely to find you feel highly stressed.

	NOT IMPORTANT	IMPORTANT
URGENT	Things that are urgent but not really important could be delegated to someone else to do	Spending too much of your time doing things that are important and have become urgent feels highly stressful
NOT URGENT	If you are spending time doing things that are neither important nor urgent – STOP!	Spending most of your time doing things that are important but not yet urgent helps you to feel in control

Step 6: Make some changes to how you schedule your time. There are many tools that you can use to help you to schedule your time effectively. There are no right or wrong ones but it is important that you identify the tools that work for you. These could include a diary, a day book, a wall planner/white board, to do lists and mobile apps.

The following checklist will help you to use whichever scheduling tool you have selected effectively:

- Ensure you understand the purpose of your job and are really focused on it.

- Schedule in progress tasks first, i.e. tasks that help you to make progress towards the achievement of a business target or goal; ask yourself what you need to achieve today/this week/this month.

- Then build in time for maintenance tasks, i.e. tasks that you have to do because they keep things ticking over.

- Build in thinking and planning time, and preparation time for meetings.

- Build in some contingency for interruptions (because there will be some).

- If the task is large, break it into sub tasks and schedule the various parts of it.

- Establish priorities by considering whether tasks are urgent and/or important.

- Avoid lots of very short periods (five minutes here and there); schedule a more continuous stretch of time.

- Set deadlines and targets but allow yourself enough time to complete a task.

- Schedule difficult and important jobs when you are at your best time of day.

- Aim to achieve something that moves your business forward every day.

- Make a daily/weekly to do list and refer to it.

- Organise others around you.

- Frequently ask yourself, 'Is what I'm doing the best use of my time right now?' and don't be afraid to simply stop doing something if your answer is 'No!'

Chapter 8

MANAGING COMMERCIAL
RISK IN AN EARLY
YEARS BUSINESS

This chapter is going to focus on risk management within an early years business. You will, of course, be familiar with the need to manage health and safety risks in your setting and will, I am sure, have detailed and robust policies and procedures in place to ensure the safeguarding of the children in your care. But have you given equal consideration to the commercial risks faced by your early years business, i.e. the things that could put your business at risk?

'We're just a small charity – does commercial risk apply to my setting?'

Even if your setting is a registered charity you are still classed as a business in many respects and are faced with the same sort of commercial risks as any other business. As such, there are various things that can go wrong – this is all I mean when I talk about business (or commercial) risks. As a trustee of a registered charity, you have a legal responsibility to try to prevent them from happening, or to minimise the negative consequences if they can't be prevented. You hold the charity in trust for current and future beneficiaries.

The Charity Commission acknowledges this responsibility and confirms on its website:

> Identifying and managing the possible and probable risks that a charity might face over its working life is a key part of effective governance for charities of all sizes and complexity...

> Trustees of smaller charities...are encouraged to make a risk
> management statement as a matter of good practice.[1]

Remember that as a trustee, you can be held liable for your setting's debts or other liabilities if you act unlawfully or negligently. Trustees act jointly when running a charity, so the trustees as a group would be liable to repay any losses. In effect you are each responsible for each other. Trustees can also be liable if your charity has any debts which it can't pay from its money or assets, for example, to suppliers, funders or staff.

The Charity Commission can take trustees to court to recover funds lost to their charity (classed as a breach of trust). This means trustees can be sued personally to recover any money owed and can be the subject of law suits, for example, in situations where poor procedures result in a health and safety breach. It is therefore essential that you take reasonable steps to reduce and manage such risks.

So, do ensure that trustees are given a role description that sets out clearly that trustees are responsible for overseeing the setting's financial resources. Trustees should:

- ensure there is enough money coming in so the setting can continue to operate sustainably

- monitor income and spending

- approve the annual financial statement and budget

- ensure there is insurance to protect the setting from liabilities

- participate in fundraising

- ensure legal compliance.

Identifying the risks affecting your early years business

The first step in managing commercial risks is to make sure that you understand what the risks are that could affect your early years business and how serious a risk they are to you.

---

1   See page 10 on www.gov.uk/government/uploads/system/uploads/attachment_
     data/file/509704/cc26_lowink.pdf

Working through the following steps will help you to create a document called a Risk Register which you can use alongside your Early Years Business Dashboard to measure your performance and progress in each of the areas of your dashboard and to manage those where there are risks.

RAG rating explained

The easiest way to quantify risks is to use a system of RAG rating. This involves using a traffic light system of red for danger/the most serious risks, amber for moderate risks and green for the risks that are under control.

A RAG rating is made up of a combination of two things:

• how likely is it that a problem will arise

• how serious a problem would this be to your business if it were to arise.

So it typically looks like this:

		Impact			
		1 (MINOR)	2 (MODERATE)	3 (SIGNIFICANT)	4 (CATASTROPHIC)
Likelihood	4 (HIGHLY LIKELY)	Amber	Amber	Red	Red
	3 (LIKELY)	Green	Amber	Red	Red
	2 (POSSIBLE)	Green	Green	Amber	Red
	1 (UNLIKELY)	Green	Green	Amber	Amber

So let's return to your Early Years Business Dashboard (which I hope you completed when you read Chapter 1) and work through a couple of examples so you can see what your Risk Register might look like in a few areas.

Financial						
Area of risk	Target	Nature of risk	Likelihood	Impact	RAG rating	Action to be taken
Revenue/ turnover	£220,000 by end of financial year	Insufficient revenue generated	3	2	Amber	• Review fee rates • Increase marketing

Quality						
Area of risk	Target	Nature of risk	Likelihood	Impact	RAG rating	Action to be taken
Ofsted grade	Retain GOOD grade	Loss of GOOD grade	2	3	Amber	• Conduct mock Ofsted

Staff						
Area of risk	Target	Nature of risk	Likelihood	Impact	RAG rating	Action to be taken
Retain an effective committee	Recruit to fill all vacancies	Unable to recruit new committee members	4	3	Red	• Review legal structure
Staff qualifications	6 Level 3 qualified staff by March	Staff fail to achieve their L3 qualification	1	2	Green	• Ask assessors to confirm staff on track to achieve L3

So take some time to return to your Early Years Business Dashboard and make a list of all the possible risks attached to the targets that you set yourself for your business. Be honest when you are doing this. There's no point doing this if you're tempted to sugar-coat the situation.

Actions to reduce and manage commercial risk

This next section will help you to consider possible actions that you might like to consider taking to reduce and manage commercial risks within your early years business.

Incorporation

We considered legal structures back in Chapter 3 of this book so I'm not going to repeat all of that content. However, I would like to provide a quick reminder about how this impacts on your exposure to commercial risk.

The following legal structures leave a high level of exposure to personal risk for those involved in running early years businesses. Despite this, they are legal structures that are still in common use and often without the various parties having a full understanding of the risks they may face.

- *Sole trader* – all risk sits with the sole trader themselves and can result in personal property, e.g. your home, being subject to claims by creditors

- *Unincorporated partnerships* – the same situation as for a sole trader, except that the risk is shared with other partners

- *Registered charity* – here the trustees (or to use the language of our sector – the committee members) are considered to be 'jointly and severally' liable for all risks and claims against the business

- *Unincorporated associations or clubs* – this informal structure carries the same risks as those mentioned above with anyone who has signed up to a committee taking on liability.

The following legal structures, referred to as incorporated (as opposed to unincorporated), can be used to limit the liability of individuals to commercial risks involved in the running of your business:

- Private Limited Company (limited by shares or by guarantee)

- Limited Liability Partnership

- Charitable Incorporated Organisation (CIO)

- Community Interest Company (CIC).

Business planning

A business plan provides a business sat-nav to keep your early years business on track. This can help you understand what the business is doing well and what you would like it to do better, and also supports the business through the process of making improvements and implementing change.

Just like a sat-nav for your car, in order to be effective, it should be regularly referred to, reviewed and updated as things change (your sat-nav is no help to you if it remains locked in the glove compartment of your car).

Your business plan should be in writing – not just in someone's head. This enables you to share it with others such as staff. Your Early Years Business Dashboard and the analysis that underpins it should form a key part of your business plan.

A robust business plan should include a financial forecast that: lists expected income from all sources, for example, funding, fees, fundraising, and all expected expenditure; shows how the business will cope with seasonal peaks and troughs, for example, in September when numbers of children tend to be lower; and indicates how your income and expenditure would be affected in the future by changes such as implementation of the 30 hours free entitlement.

Contracts

You should have written contracts with a range of people and organisations that your early years business comes into contact with, this includes:

- your local authority and any other funders, e.g., Big Lottery

- parents and carers

- staff and volunteers

- suppliers

- partners (e.g., other early years providers who work with you to provide services such as childminders who provide your out of hours provision)

- landlords.

Some contracts may be a legal requirement, for example, staff employment contracts. Check who your business has contracts with. Are you missing any that you should have?

Premises issues for early years businesses

Some of the risks and challenges involved in finding suitable premises to support the current and future needs of your early years business are not to be underestimated. The following checklist can be used to help you to think through the various factors involved in choosing suitable premises for your setting. Considering these points will also help to minimise risks associated with your premises.

- The basics:
  - » well lit, ideally with plenty of sources of natural light
  - » an adequate temperature all year round and properly ventilated
  - » clean and well-maintained
  - » adequate space for the children attending, and also space for storing equipment
  - » ideally outdoor space to facilitate free-flow activity
- Legal:
  - » premises agreements may take one of the following forms but should ensure you have security of tenure – typical agreements might include:
    - — *Hire agreement* – an agreement to use a specific area of a shared building for a set number of days and a set number of hours (typically used in village halls or other community facilities). Notice to quit could be given at short notice (potentially a week) and so this is not a secure arrangement and can also be quite costly. The landlord retains many of the responsibilities for the building/premises and may not allow any alterations to be made. Storage can be an issue as nothing can remain in the area once the users have finished and all equipment etc. has to be stored. Can also include use of an outdoor area/ kitchen, etc.
    - — *Licence* – an agreement to use a defined area of a shared building at set times/days. This is usually in

place for an agreed number of years. Can be used for village halls etc. and offers more security than a hire agreement. Depending on the premises, you may be allowed to leave equipment etc. out in the areas of use. The user will usually have some responsibility for maintenance. Alterations may be permissible by agreement. There may also be break clauses at certain intervals. This agreement can also include use of an outdoor area.

— *Lease* – this agreement will stipulate conditions for the lease of a whole premises for a set period. There are terms of use of the premises and the user will usually be responsible for internal maintenance (check what this includes – I had a client who ended up in dispute with their landlords over whether window frames were internal or external). There may be clauses to allow subletting or this may be restricted. This agreement can also include an outdoor area. Alterations may be permissible by agreement. This offers most security. Can also be a land lease.

• Space:

» Space for physical activity allowing children to move and to work on a large scale, both alone and with others.

» Space to set up the environment to encourage independence and a sense of responsibility.

» Carry out regular observation of how children are using the space and make changes to improve the environment, e.g., in one setting staff noted that some children were overwhelmed by the congestion created by all the coat pegs being close to the door. The setting simply moved the coat pegs further down the corridor, and staggered the arrival time by five minutes for the first half term allowing new children to arrive first and get settled before the older children arrived. This created more space and reduced the stress of arriving for the newer children (and their parents) and helped children to settle much more easily into the day.

» Ensure a suitable place is available for parents and staff to talk in private (so many staff supervisions are conducted in broom cupboards).

» Ensure children who need additional support in accessing the curriculum are catered for, e.g., a setting may have to widen its doorways to make wheelchair access easier.

- Safety and security:

  » Make children's safety a priority within your health and safety policy.

  » Appoint a senior person as having responsibility for ensuring the policy is implemented.

  » Conduct rigorous risk assessment for all of your activities identifying any significant risks, such as lifting/carrying a child or the use of hazardous substances, and who might be harmed, including staff, children, or visitors to your setting.

  » Produce a plan with clear steps to minimise risks, including regular monitoring.

  » Provide appropriate safety information, effective controls and training for all staff (plus briefing for any visitors to your setting).

  » An accident reporting and investigation system aimed at preventing recurrences should also be in place.

There are many organisations which provide information about health and safety for small businesses including:

» The Health and Safety Executive (HSE) infoline provides confidential, practical free advice.

» The Royal Society for the Prevention of Accidents (RoSPA) provides an advice pack.

» The Institution of Occupational Safety and Health (IOSH) offers a risk management toolkit.

Succession planning

A succession plan sets out the steps you are taking to ensure key roles in your early years business (including volunteers on your Committee) are filled and not left vacant, now and in the foreseeable future. It should include planning for future expansion and changes in the business, for example changes to opening hours, as well as assuming that staff might leave at some point.

As with all of the plans that I have mentioned in this book, your succession plan should be in writing and be specific, not just some vague thoughts in your head.

You should base your succession plan on information you get through having regular discussions with staff about their plans for the future, as well as your plans for the business.

Well established recruitment and selection procedures will support a succession plan, as will a training and development plan designed to develop multi-skilled staff who can cover each other's roles, as well as more competent staff who can take on more senior roles in the future.

So for each key role in your business set out what you would do immediately if the current job holder was suddenly unavailable to you, and what you would do in the longer term to replace that person.

Business continuity planning

A business continuity plan sets out how your early years business would continue to operate if disaster struck. There is evidence that businesses that have a business continuity plan in place are more likely to survive a crisis. Because of this, having a business continuity plan in place builds the confidence of official organisations, such as local authorities, Ofsted, banks, etc. Such a plan is often an expectation now for businesses who are applying for funding. Having a business continuity plan makes good sense – it's about being prepared for emergencies. Typical risks to consider within your business continuity plan include things like:

- premises related issues such as fire, flood, extreme weather, failure of utilities resulting in inability to heat or light your premises, being denied access to your premises, e.g. due to a gas leak

- staff related issues such as loss of a key staff member through death, long term illness or resignation, sudden loss of large numbers of staff through pandemics, mass resignations, e.g. following a big lottery win or poaching by a new competitor

- computer failure/cyber crime

- key suppliers letting you down, e.g. transport

- financial issues such as changes to government funding policy resulting in loss of income, fraud, being sued

- closure by regulators due to an incident or serious complaint.

For each of the risks that you identify, consider how your business would cope in these situations and have a go at completing a plan using this format.

Risk (describe the risk)	Severity		Action plan
	How likely is it that this will happen?	If it does, how serious would the impact be?)	
Example: Premises broken into and some damage has occurred	Low – we are in a secure location	High - Forced to close one of our rooms for a week in order to make repairs resulting in lack of space for children to attend the setting	1. Get alarm system installed and ensure regular servicing – train staff on how to set it 2. Get quote for CCTV 3. Review insurance policies for business continuity cover

Once you have created your business continuity plan it should be communicated with everyone who might be affected and updated regularly. It should be stored safely – with copies available in an accessible location off-site in case you can't get into your premises to retrieve it. And, like any good plan, it should be tested (just like doing a fire drill).

The London Prepared website provides some excellent free tools that businesses can download to assist with business continuity planning (and you don't have to be based in London to benefit from them).[2]

Insurance

The purpose of insurance is to protect you and your early years business against risks that you may not be able to prevent from occurring. It is possible to insure against virtually anything, with Lloyds brokers specialising in covering all sorts of risks, but I'm going to concentrate here on the main sorts of business insurance that you might want to consider purchasing.

In our sector, once your business has signed a contract with a local authority to provide childcare services, you are legally obliged to do so, regardless of changes to your circumstances. The risks highlighted previously may make it difficult for your setting to continue to provide childcare services if something goes wrong. Sometimes nothing can be done to prevent a crisis from occurring, so it makes sense to take out insurance against those risks.

The following types of insurance are a legal requirement.

Employer's liability insurance

This is required by law (under the Compulsory Insurance Act 1969) to provide cover in the event that one of your staff members is injured or becomes ill as a result of working for you. Most policies provide £10 million of cover. There is a requirement for your policy certificate to be on display or otherwise accessible to staff. Certificates should be retained as it is possible for an employee to make a claim against your employer's liability insurance many years in the future and you might need to know who your business was covered by at that time. An example of this would be an employee who many years after working for you develops a lung condition caused by exposure to asbestos during the time that they worked for you. This is currently an issue for a number of employers where older public buildings such as schools and village halls have been found to have damaged areas of asbestos where staff are working. If you are a childminder trading as a limited company where you are the only employee (as a director of the business) Employer's Liability Insurance is still required.

---

2   www.london.gov.uk/about-us/organisations-we-work/london-prepared/preparing-your-business

Vehicle insurance

All drivers are required by law (under the Road Traffic Act of 1930) to have in force an insurance policy to cover their liability for bodily injury to or damage to third party property which arises from the use of a motor vehicle. The cover does not have to be anything other than Third Party only although many policies are now arranged on a Third Party Fire and Theft or Fully Comprehensive basis. If you use your own vehicle for business purposes, for example, if you run an after school club and pick up children from school or you are a childminder, your personal vehicle insurance must include use of your vehicle for business purposes.

The following insurance is not required by law but may be required by the EYFS or by your local authority in order for you to offer early years and childcare services:

Public liability insurance

This covers compensation claims made against you for injury, or for damage to someone's property by any third party such as parents, children, suppliers, or any other member of the public who comes into contact with your business. An example would be if you have play equipment on the floor and a visitor to your setting trips over it; they could sue you for the injury they've suffered. Compensation payments can be high as they can take into account things like medical bills, lost income and legal fees. Your public liability insurance would cover these costs, up to the limit of your policy. Your local authority contract may require you to have in place at least £5 million of public liability cover. This is also applicable if you operate your early years business from your home, as is the case for childminders.

Building and contents insurance

This provides financial protection if your property is damaged through events like burglary, fire or flooding.

Business interruption insurance is usually offered as an extra when you buy buildings or contents insurance and will cover you for any periods when you cannot operate as normal because of an event resulting in damage to your premises, such as your boiler breaking down in the middle of winter. Business interruption insurance will pay an amount to cover the shortfall in profit, and pays any increased costs of running your business as a result of the event (for example, renting alternative premises for a period of time after a flood). If somebody else owns the building your setting operates from, you should check with the owner that the building is insured. If you operate your setting from home, for example, as a childminder, you should make sure your home insurance covers your business activities.

Trustee indemnity insurance

The Charity Commission recommends trustee indemnity insurance for committee-run settings. This covers trustees from having to personally pay legal claims made against them in their capacity as trustees. As it benefits individual trustees, you would need proper legal authority in your constitution before you can pay for it using the charity's money (alternatively trustees can buy their own), but remember to read the small print very carefully – trustee indemnity insurance usually won't pay out if there is evidence of negligence, for example, poor financial management resulting in losses causing the setting to file for bankruptcy, or injury to a child as a result of inadequate safeguarding arrangements. So it's really important that you don't rely on insurance as a means of protecting trustees in a situation where your committee is not fulfilling its functions effectively.

Legal expenses insurance

This covers the cost of pursuing legal action or defending your business against legal action where this isn't covered by your liability insurance, for example, in an employment tribunal. The insurance will cover fees for solicitors, barristers, accountants, etc., as well as court costs if you are ordered to pay them. Legal expenses insurers often provide advice and a legal helpline. You may find that this sort of insurance is included as a membership benefit if you belong to a professional or trade organisation.

There are a few other sorts of insurance that may only be relevant in certain circumstances if you engage in certain activities.

Professional indemnity insurance

Professional indemnity (PI) insurance is only relevant to you if you contract to provide advice to other settings about how to operate their early years business. Informal mentoring arrangements would not imply a liability. PI insurance, as it is known, can help protect you against claims made for so-called 'business injury' if you were to provide advice that proved to be wrong, incorrect or in some other way damaging to their business.

Product liability insurance

If you supply goods, for example, selling a range of early learning equipment to parents, there's always the possibility that the product could cause damage to a third party. Product liability insurance covers you for this risk.

Other staff insurance

There are some types of insurance that you can take out which would ultimately benefit your employees and so might cause them to incur a tax liability as a Benefit in Kind. This includes things like life insurance, private medical insurance and income protection insurance. These are seldom provided by early years businesses but are common elsewhere in the corporate world.

The Association of British Insurers provides information on its website about the types of business insurance that you might need.

Where to buy insurance

Your first port of call should be any professional bodies or trade associations that you belong to as most have a relationship with certain insurers which offer discounts to their members. In some cases you might even find that some of the insurances mentioned above are included as a part of your membership of that organisation.

Insurance comparison sites make it easy to compare costs and most these days include business insurance as a part of their service. However, they are only really suitable if you are pretty confident about what you need.

Insurance brokers will help you if you are not sure what you need or if your needs are complex. You can find out if an insurance broker is authorised by checking on the Financial Conduct Authority website.[3]

Confirming other people's insurance

Let's turn this around for a moment and think about insurance from the point of view of other people and organisations that your early years business comes into contact with. This might include your landlord, agencies who provide supply cover, and businesses who supply products and services to you. It is worth checking when you contract with any of these organisations that they have adequate insurance cover and asking to see a copy of their latest insurance certificates. Repeat this regularly to ensure they keep their cover up to date.

Fraud prevention

Fraud can be defined as any situation where money is taken by deception or without authorisation. Fraud can and does occur in the physical world – the traditional idea of someone having their fingers in the till and taking cash. But more frequently these days fraud is perpetrated using digital methods including online banking, false accounting and in other ways deliberately falsifying financial records in order to divert money away from the business. Over the past couple of years I have supported clients dealing with:

- An office administrator who was adding items of her own personal shopping onto the setting's supermarket shopping bill (which she was responsible for arranging). This was only discovered when she went on maternity leave and, following investigation, was found to have been going on for years. As a long-standing and trusted member of staff, employed by the business since it started, no one had checked the shopping receipts before she entered the information into the accounts. It was done quite carefully so as not to draw attention to the fraud with usually two of the same items being purchased when only one was required by the setting.

---

3   www.fca.org.uk/firms/financial-services-register

- The trustee appointed as treasurer of a committee-run setting perpetrating a major fraud resulting in the theft through online banking of tens of thousands of pounds leaving the setting insolvent. This fraud had been accomplished through the creation by that person of false accounts. The other trustees had relied on this person, who was financially qualified, and had not bothered to check the accounts being presented at committee meetings against the bank statements.

In early years businesses, trustees, committee members, governors and business owners can all be held liable for debts incurred by the business, even where fraud has taken place, so strong financial systems to protect against fraud are essential. And as mentioned previously, trustee indemnity insurance is unlikely to pay out if there is evidence that negligence by the trustees contributed towards the fraud being perpetrated. Failure to cross check information being presented by an employee or a volunteer, as in the cases outlined above, would be viewed as negligence.

According to Action Fraud,[4] good fraud prevention procedures include:

- making sure that pre-employment checks ask referees about the honesty of the employee (and also applying this procedure to volunteers on your committee)

- stating clearly in your employment policies that you have a zero tolerance culture in relation to dishonesty and that any cases discovered would be treated as gross misconduct

- watching out for changes in the behaviour of your staff – the obvious things like suddenly being able to afford a foreign holiday and also the less obvious like a staff member being reluctant to take time off or to delegate financial tasks to someone else

- whistle-blowing policies that encourage staff and volunteers to report any concerns they may have about another person involved with the setting, even if that person is senior to them and in a position of authority

---

4   www.actionfraud.police.uk/

- robust processes and controls to ensure the activities of one person are checked, signed off or audited by a second person.

Fraud can also be carried out by people from outside your business, particularly through hacking into your various accounts so put into place good online security as I outlined earlier.

Finally, if fraud is detected, do not delay involving the police as, however difficult this may feel, this may be an expectation of any insurance policies that you have in place.

Planning to exit the business

There comes a point in most businesses when the people who set it up and guided it to a position of success wish to (or need to) step down and hand over the reins to someone else. This can be a high risk time for an early years business, with many failing to make the transition successfully to new ownership.

Inevitably, the less time you have to plan your exit from the business, the more hazardous that is likely to be for the business. So, unforeseen circumstances such as the death of an owner or sudden ill health can have catastrophic consequences. I recall speaking to a setting owner who had previously run the setting with her husband. Following his sudden death, she suddenly found that she couldn't even gain access to the company bank accounts to pay staff, as no planning or preparation had been done to cope with this unfortunate event. This resulted in the closure of the setting (temporarily). I never got to hear if she actually managed to get it up and running again.

Earlier in the chapter, I discussed business continuity planning and succession planning, and a part of your planning process must be to consider how you plan to exit the business. Don't get into the situation of one setting manager I met who, at our first meeting at a network event, informed me that she was 67 and really wanted to retire. I was surprised to bump into her again at another network meeting a year later. 'You're still here', I commented. 'Yes', she said with a sigh, 'I'm still trying to figure out how to retire but no one else in the setting wants to run it'. And guess what – there she still was a year on at the same network meeting – at which point I suggested we sit down and figure out a plan to support her exit. A year on I was rather disappointed when I bumped into her again, but this time she was smiling, 'I'm here as a volunteer this year'. Part of her exit strategy had been to provide mentoring support to her deputy by offering to continue to support the setting as a volunteer until the deputy found her feet. I wished her a happy retirement.

In other situations the answer may be to sell the business, which, if it is a private nursery, may prove to be a lucrative option. Again preparation is essential. Just as if you were selling your house, you'd have a tidy up, make essential repairs and give it a lick of paint, taking a couple of years to shape the business so that it offers an attractive and enticing option for people and organisations who are in the market to buy a nursery is time well spent.

Christie and Co, who specialise in brokering the sale and acquisition of early years businesses, advise that buyers of early years businesses typically look for:

- high quality freehold or leasehold settings

- settings with a minimum of 50 places

- proven and established levels of earnings and opportunities for further development

- businesses which have been subject to ongoing capital expenditure and investment

- Good or Outstanding Ofsted outcomes

- settings that employ a highly qualified, well remunerated workforce.

So if you are thinking about selling your early years business at some point over the coming years, use this as your preparation checklist to get it into good shape to be attractive to buyers.

Partnership working

For many early years businesses the introduction by the government of new initiatives, such as the 30 hours offer, can feel like a major threat. And they certainly can be if you attempt to tackle them alone. The 30 hours initiative is one of those changes that has created a significant opportunity for early years businesses to reduce their individual exposure to commercial risk by working collaboratively in partnership with other providers.

There is much good practice emerging in relation to partnership working within the sector, with hubs being created around schools, and effective partnerships drawing in a range of diverse providers such as pre-schools, childminders, schools and out of school settings.

In this section I'm going to outline some good practice in relation to partnership working based around a model originally devised by the Roffey Park Institute in 2005. I have adapted this model and introduced it to many of the early years businesses I have supported over the years, resulting in some highly effective and supportive partnerships being created.

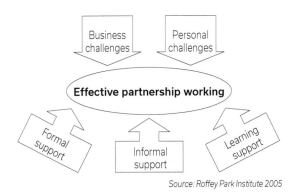

Source: Roffey Park Institute 2005

Business challenges

Selecting the right partners in a business relationship is similar to selecting the right partner in life. My mum used to say 'marry in haste, repent at your leisure' and the same is true here. Choosing an inappropriate partner to work with may result in a relationship that is blighted by cultural differences and political tensions, and which ultimately cause the partnership to fail.

We might be tempted to simply decide to partner with other providers with whom we have an existing relationship without realising that moving to work in a partnership model may change the dynamic of that relationship. Again, likening this to our personal lives, a partner who we enjoy dating may not be the most appropriate person for us to marry.

Beginning a conversation about working in partnership means that both parties will need to enter into a process of due diligence which allows both to explore your similarities, your differences, and ultimately your suitability for each other. So, before entering into this sort of dialogue it is essential that you have thought carefully about the things that really matter to you, that you wouldn't be prepared to compromise on – what I call your non-negotiables. In one setting I am currently working with this has included things like:

- all partners share vision and values

- continue to offer an exciting and active curriculum that seeks to inspire and enthuse children's thirst for learning

- the setting to retain its own committee with representation from parents

- the setting to retain its branding and name

- the manager to remain in charge of the day to day operations and running of the setting, and all decisions affecting the setting, staff and children

- the partnership to encourage the setting's independence and individuality and not require conforming to one way

- a genuine partnership without one partner dictating to others

- that collaborative working with other local settings outside of the partnership can be maintained

- opportunities for sharing of resources and ideas to continue to improve what each setting can offer

- bonds with the community, church, etc.

- keep an active parent involvement, e.g. open door, events, parent helpers

- a commitment by all partners to high-quality CPD to support all staff

- partnering with other good or outstanding settings so that the setting can continue to focus on the areas where it needs to improve rather than being drawn into helping out poorly performing settings.

Working in partnership involves overcoming business challenges. Actions to support this might include practical things like finding workable mechanisms for managing the partnership and deciding how to get things done when decisions need to be referred elsewhere. Communicating and meeting in ways that are mutually convenient is often a challenge – this can be a particular issue, for example, where schools (whose staff are keen to meet during the school day) are working in partnership with childminders (who may find that impossible).

Personal challenges

As well as the business challenges, creating an effective partnership also involves overcoming a number of personal challenges in order to establish trust between partners. These challenges might include:

- being prepared to live with ambiguity – it may be unclear for staff and parents for a while just how it's going to work

- a sense of frustration as things can take time to move forward and get sorted out

- balancing conflicting demands – working in partnership will involve making compromises, including dedicating some time and effort to supporting the partnership which may take you away from your own setting at times

- working with cultural differences – the classic 'we don't do it like that' may well rear its head and need to be tackled sensitively.

Formal support

There are a number of mechanisms that can be put into place to support the development of an effective partnership and give it a good chance of being successful. I've outlined these using headings from the 7S Analysis model that I introduced in Chapter 2.

Strategy – reaching agreement

- A shared vision for the partnership

- Principles to be applied

- Joint business planning

- Leadership teams working together with the establishment maybe of a Partnership Governance Team

- Clear lines of accountability that set out who is ultimately responsible for what.

Structure – putting it in place

- Management, teams and staff

- Deciding how to make best use of premises

- Deciding which of the partners will be responsible for customer relationship management

- Data management and sharing.

Systems – ensuring compatibility

- Financial forecasting systems

- Project planning and management

- Monitoring and reporting progress and outcomes of children (do we use different tools?)

- Internal communication arrangements

- Marketing and branding (will the partnership have its own brand?)

- Shared standards for quality management

- IT compatibility (will our systems talk to each other?).

Staffing – getting the right people involved

- Getting the right people around the table to lead the partnership

- Managers who can operate as transformational leaders to support change – a high level of management visibility is essential

- Staff who buy-in to the shared values and collective vision

- Staff who can cope with ambiguity – many questions will remain unanswered until things are fully up and running

- Staff being flexible potentially allowing staff to be shared

- Succession planning for the future.

Informal support – making the relationship work

The Roffey Park team state that, 'Formal processes can provide the scaffolding for effective collaborative working but personal relationships are just as important in overcoming the challenges' (Hirsh, Garrow and Holbeche 2005). So formal processes as outlined above only go so far in making a partnership work effectively. The softer things matter just as much. This might include things like:

- agreeing shared values

- identifying common ground

- establishing strong relationships in key positions

- using informal contact, e.g., having a meal together, as well as formal meetings – teams that play together stay together

- being open and discussing problems as soon as they arise and establishing ground rules for resolving problems – so that business problems don't become personal ones.

Learning support – being committed to learning together how to make the partnership work

It's essential to recognise and openly acknowledge that this way of working is new to everyone and that you're all learning together how best to make it work. So it's important to develop and communicate widely:

- a thorough understanding of the partnership's purpose

- an understanding of each other's business and the overall offering

- awareness of the challenges of collaborative working and reassure that these can be overcome.

This will require leaders who have excellent influencing, interpersonal and negotiation skills and who are able to mediate and resolve conflict, to anticipate and plan for problems and to manage change.

Remember, any partnership is only as strong as weakest link. It is only through embracing this that you will truly capitalise on the value of synergy where your partnership offer to parents and children becomes of greater value than the sum of all the individual parts.

Chapter 9

TAKING THE PAIN OUT OF CHANGE

After everything that you have read about in the preceding chapters of this book, you may have come to the conclusion that you need to make some changes in your early years business in order for it to become more successful. If your plan is to grow your early years business then planning for change is essential – any growth you engage with will always involves change. And I'm sure that you will agree with John Kotter's assertion that 'The rate of change is not going to slow down anytime soon. If anything, competition… will probably speed up even more in the next few decades' (Kotter 2002, p.130).

The actions you need to take to support your plans for future growth take into account many of the factors covered in this and previous chapters. This chapter will help you to consider how change takes place in a business and how to introduce changes into your early years business with less pain and greater success. Make sure that you consider some of this when you create the Continuous Improvement section of your Early Years Business Dashboard.

Not all change is the same

There are different types of change that you might need to consider making. This simple model helps you to think about them and to determine how best to deal with them.

	Incremental change	Transformational change
Proactive	Fine tuning	Transformation
Reactive	Adaptation	Disruption

Fine tuning

Fine tuning is the type of change that involves you making small or incremental changes to something that you already do, and doing this because you have decided that it's a good idea. No one is forcing you to do it – you are doing it proactively. An example of this might be where you have reviewed the way in which you set out your rooms and have decided that you could use your space more effectively by moving things around. This type of change is pretty easy to make and usually experiences few barriers. Because this is the simplest form of change to deal with it is often a good idea to try to move other forms of change into this realm.

Adaptation

Adaptation also involves small amounts of incremental change, but is change that is required of you by some external force. This could be, for example, small changes to the Ofsted framework, or feedback from a parent about how they would like you to support their child, or a new system for reporting your attendance numbers introduced by the local authority. This type of change feels manageable, but may be more challenging to implement if staff don't understand the importance of doing it. It is often said 'People don't resist change. They resist being changed! It is the sense of change being forced onto people that makes it feel uncomfortable.

Making this form of change easier to implement means anticipating what's coming up. Keeping abreast of proposed changes to the Ofsted framework, for example, would mean that you could proactively introduce the changes required well before any deadline is set by the regulator.

Transformation

Moving over to the right hand side of the model brings us to transformational change. This is change that involves more than a few tweaks and minor improvements. Transformational change usually involves larger scale changes that you have decided to make yourself, such as move to new premises or opening a second setting, and also changes that may impact on the culture of the business and how people will be expected to work.

Because this type of change is larger scale it often feels more challenging to implement; it can take much longer and so can lose momentum and requires considerable planning to make it happen.

Making this form of change feel more manageable means breaking it down into bite-sized chunks; the classic idea of eating an elephant one bite at a time. This means careful planning and setting realistic timescales so that various elements of the change can be completed before moving onto the next. In reality this can sometimes be difficult to achieve.

Disruption

By far the most challenging form of change is large scale, transformational change which is imposed upon us by some outside force. In recent times, this sort of change has become known as disruptive change. Outside our sector, examples of this that are having a massive impact on other industries include the emergence of Uber and its impact on licensed taxis (many of whom are going out of business), and the massive growth of online shopping which is changing the face of our high streets completely.

In our sector business disruption is caused by a number of external factors including increased competition from schools entering into the early years market, government initiatives such as the introduction of the 30 hours entitlement and major changes to the funding and qualification requirement for early years apprenticeships.

Making this sort of change more palatable may mean moving it towards the left – by breaking it down into smaller chunks, or by keeping a close eye on possible changes so that you can make your preparations for them sooner rather than later. In Chapter 2 I discussed the PESTLE Analysis. This is the tool that I would recommend you to use on a regular basis to help you to anticipate and begin to plan for future disruptive influences that might impact on your early years business.

Why people find change painful

Despite the fact that constant change has become a reality in most people's working lives it is still something that many people find difficult to cope with. This is because change involves coping with things that, as human beings, we find particularly tricky. Change is about coping with endings, transitions and beginnings.

Endings

When we are faced with change this inevitably means us having to come to terms with letting go of the old. Doing this often creates a sense of loss even if what we have to get rid of is something that we know is no longer fit for purpose. It's like throwing away a favourite pair of shoes that are so past their best that they are falling to pieces and no longer water tight. Because they are comfortable and familiar, we somehow manage to convince ourselves that we can still find a use for them (like only wearing them when it's not been raining). Our reluctance to let go of the old can be a barrier to change.

Transitions

As you will know, because you support children through them, transitions are times when we are likely to be faced with ambiguity, and a certain amount of confusion and chaos. Just these words are enough to send many of us into a quiver. The anxiety we feel about uncertainty can cause us to question how we will fit it to a new way of working and to question our ability to make the changes needed. A crisis of self-esteem can often accompany a period of transition so again we tend to reach out to what we feel confident in and hold onto that for dear life as if it were a life jacket. During a period of transition we also spend a lot of our time wondering what the new way of working will be like. This involves exploring options, alternatives and possibilities and, although it can be quite a positive experience, it does tend to occupy a lot of our time and become the focus of our attention.

Beginnings

Many of us find new things very motivational but for some they are stressful experiences. New beginnings involve coming to terms with new realities which might require us to think and behave differently. We may need to rethink what's important to us and to embrace new goals. And we will most certainly need to experience new ways of working in order to develop our competence and confident in the new context.

So it is human nature to feel resistant to change, especially change that we feel is being forced upon us.

You may have come across the change curve, which has over the years been adapted from Elizabeth Kübler-Ross's original model to support bereavement and grief. This is a very useful way of portraying how people often react when faced with change.

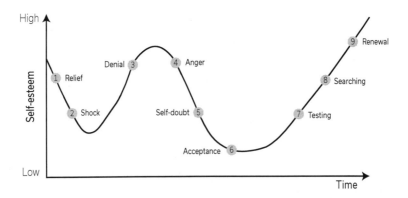

The change curve, which originates from the world of grief counselling, illustrates the natural journey that we tend to go through when faced with change. So, when you are planning to make a change in your setting, think in advance about how you can best support and guide your staff through the change curve.

A lot of the time telling people the right things at the right time can be a big help in supporting them. I like to use Ken Blanchard's Sticky Change model as it provides a really good sequence that you can use to support staff through change and ensure that the changes you introduce actually stick. Below is the sequence, which is based on what he calls the six stages of concern that people have about change. It's really important to cover points in this order (which we often don't, with the consequence that people feel uncomfortable with change).

Stage 1. Information concerns – it's important to make sure people are clear about the change before moving on, otherwise they are left wondering what's going to happen and can't move on from that – this early stage is also your opportunity to inspire them about the change so bear in mind this quote which is often attributed to Saint Exupery, the author of the lovely book *The Little Prince*: 'If you want to build a ship do not gather men together and assign tasks. Instead teach them the longing for the wide endless sea'. Help them to see your vision for how the change you are proposing will improve things for children, parents and staff:

- What is the change that's being made?

- Why is it needed?

- What's wrong with the way things are now?

- How much does the business need to change?

Stage 2. Personal concerns – once people understand what's changing, their concerns are focused on themselves; if we fail to address their personal concerns they will worry and become stressed about the change and won't be able to move on from that:

- How will this change affect me personally?

- How will I benefit? (What's in it for me?)

- Will I be disadvantaged in any way?

- How much time will it take for me to implement this change?

- Will I need to learn new skills or do I have the necessary skills now?

Stage 3. Implementation concerns – once people have had their personal concerns addressed they are ready to think about the practicalities of making the change happen; try and cover this too soon and people are simply not ready to think about it:

- What do I do first? And what comes next?

- How will I manage all of the details?

- Who can I go to for help?

- How long will this take?

- How will the business's structure and systems and my own job change?

Stage 4. Impact concerns – change requires some effort so people naturally need to know that it's working and that it's been worthwhile; think about how you're going to measure/demonstrate this:

- Is the change making a difference?

- Are we making expected progress?

- Has the effort been worthwhile?

Stage 5. Collaboration concerns – once people accept that change is working well and was beneficial they can be asked to talk positively to others about getting involved; having to convince someone else further increases their own personal commitment to the change:

- How should we work with others to get them involved?

- How do we spread the word?

- Are there opportunities to break down silos around this change?

Stage 6. Refinement concerns – feeding people's ideas back into the continuous improvement section of your Early Years Business Dashboard ensures that they feel that they are adding value to the business:

- What ideas do you have for further improvement?

- What could we do to make things even better?

- How should we manage any future change?

Remember always that you are dealing with human beings, that people are complicated and that all sorts of things impact on our ability to cope with change. Don't assume that someone who has been very supportive of change in the past may feel the same next time. They may have other things going on in their lives that make a new change more difficult for them. And similarly, don't assume that someone who has been quite resistant to change in the past will feel the same in the future. For each new change you will have people who:

- embrace the change enthusiastically – I call these people the architects – these are the people you should involve in planning for change

- get on with implementing the change once it's been made clear to them what is required – I call these people the builders – they are the people you can rely on to get the job done

- accept change and get on board with it after a bit of persuasion and support – I call these people the dwellers – most people are probably in this category

- drag their feet and resist change – I call these people the stragglers – you may need to work quite hard with them to get them on board

- just aren't going to get there – I call these people the unmovables – whatever you do you are unlikely to shift them so you may need to decide if, ultimately, they are holding your business back.

I wouldn't use these titles to openly describe your people, but thinking about them in this way can be helpful when you are deciding how best to work with your staff through a period of change.

CLOSING THOUGHTS

If you've read my book all the way through, first of all thank you for trusting me to take you on this journey towards building your early years business. Second, well done for sticking with it.

Here is a short summary of what I have covered and what your next steps might look like.

We began in Chapter 1 by introducing the Early Years Business Dashboard as a tool to provide you with a systematic way of overseeing your business and focusing on what really matters. I hope you have now defined what needs to be in each section of your dashboard so that you can use this to keep you on track. Your next steps might include involving other members of your team in the development of more detailed action plans to take your business forward.

Chapter 2 introduced you to a selection of business analysis tools and techniques which can be used to help you to build a clear picture of the factors impacting on your early years business – both internal and external. Update your analysis once a year to keep you focused on the way ahead for your business.

In Chapter 3 I focused on the typical legal structures that might be used by early years businesses. For some of you this will have offered simply a confirmation of what you already have in place, but for others it may have thrown up questions and significant concerns about the appropriateness of your current structure. Take proper legal and financial advice before making any changes to your business. This chapter also sets out some good practice for governance and I would recommend that this is something that is of value for every early years business to think about.

It's all about the money, money, money in Chapter 4. Robust financial planning and ongoing financial management are critically important to the success of any business. However, the unique way in which the early years and childcare sector is funded makes this more challenging for businesses in our sector to operate sustainably.

In Chapter 5 I turned my focus to parents, our customers, and shared with you some thoughts about embracing new methods and new technologies to communicate with your current and prospective customers. If you've previously relied on word of mouth to fill your occupancy, perhaps look at introducing one or two new methods into your marketing plans for the coming year.

We often hear people in our sector say that we are in the people business and indeed we are. But all too often, as well as being our greatest asset, our people can end up being our biggest headache. My clients tell me that they lose more sleep over difficult people management issues than anything else. So in Chapter 6 I haven't attempted to duplicate information that is already out there and available, but rather to share with you my take on the issues and concerns that most frequently come up when clients call me for help with HR issues.

Chapter 7 deals with some of the nuts and bolts and the nitty gritty of running an early years business. Established businesses may well have most of this in place but do pause and check that what you are doing is fit for purpose, works efficiently and will support the future growth of your business. For businesses that are just starting out in the sector it provides a useful checklist of the mechanisms that you will need to put into place.

Running any business can be a risky endeavour, so Chapter 8 considers commercial risks that you should assess and, where possible, attempt to reduce. Having robust plans in place to manage in a crisis are likely to help you to get your business back on track while others without a plan might fold, meaning that valuable services for families and jobs for staff would be lost.

And finally, in case all of this feels like a bit of an upheaval, the final chapter looks at the management of change. I've called it *Taking the Pain Out of Change* because, when not managed well, change can be a very painful process for everyone involved and can cause serious disruption to a business. I hope that this chapter will help you to embrace the changes that this book has encouraged you to make with enthusiasm and excitement.

BIBLIOGRAPHY

Books

Blanchard, K. (1993) *Raving Fans!* London: Harper Collins Business.

Cope, M. (2010) *The Seven Cs of Consulting* (Third Edition). London: FT Prentice Hall,.

Herzberg, F.(1959) *The Motivation to Work.* New York: Wiley.

Hirsh, W., Garrow, V. and Holbeche, L. (2005) *Supporting Collaborative Working in Business Alliances and Partnerships.* West Sussex: Roffey Park Institute.

Kotter, J. (1996) *Leading Change.* Boston, MA: Harvard Business School Press.

Kotter, J. (2002) *The Heart of Change: Real-Life Stories of How People Change Their Organizations.* Boston, MA, Harvard Business School Press.

Kübler-Ross, E, (1969) *On Death and Dying.* New York: Macmillan.

Laborde, G.(1995) *Influencing with Integrity: Management Skills for Communication and Negotiation.* Carmarthen: Crown House Publishing.

Peters, T. and Waterman, R.H. Jnr (1982) *In Search of Excellence.* New York: Harper & Row.

University of Gloucestershire and Bates Wells and Braithwaite London LLP (2013) *Getting It Right Legally: Status and Structure for Community Organisations (GIRL1) - Playwork Partnerships.* Cheltenham: University of Gloucestershire.

University of Gloucestershire & Bates Wells and Braithwaite London LLP (2011) *Getting It Right Legally 2: Contract and Grant Relationships between Funders and Community Organisations (GIRL2) - Playwork Partnerships.* Cheltenham: University of Gloucestershire.

Articles

Jackson, L. and Fitzpatrick, K. (2013) 'Improving business skills in the early years and childcare sector.' Office for Public Management (OPM) on behalf of 4Children and the Department of Education.

Kaplan, R.S. and Norton, D. (1992) 'The Balanced Scorecard: Measures that drive performance.' *Harvard Business Review 70,* 1, 71–79.

Kaplan, R.S. and Norton, D. (1993) 'Putting the Balanced Scorecard to work.' *Harvard Business Review 71,* 5, 134–147.

Kaplan, R.S. and Norton, D. (1996') Using the Balanced Scorecard as a Strategic Management System.' *Harvard Business Review 74,* 1, 75–85.

Waterman, R.H. Jnr, Peters, T.J. and Phillips, J.R. (1980) 'Structure is not organization.' *Business Horizons 23,* 3, 14–26.

Zigarmi, P. and Hoekstra, J, (2008) Leadership Strategies for Making Change Stick – The Ken Blanchard Companies. Available at http://www.kenblanchard.com/Leading-Research/Research/Strategies-for-Making-Change-Stick, accessed 10 January 2016.

Websites

Adobe 2013 Mobile Consumer Survey http://success.adobe.com/en/na/programs/products/
     digitalmarketing/offers/june/1306-35508-mobile-consumer-survey-results.html
ACAS www.acas.org.uk - Helpline 08457 474747
Association of British Insurers (ABI) www.abi.org.uk
Bates Wells Braithewaite (BWB) http://getlegal.bwbllp.com/www.getlegal.bwbllp.com
British Insurance Brokers' Association (BIBA) www.biba.org.uk
Business Balls http://www.businessballs.com
Business in the Community ProHelp www.prohelp.org.uk
Business in You http://businessinyou.bis.gov.uk/www,businessinyou.bis.gov.uk
Chartered Institute of Personnel & Development (CIPD) www.cipd.co.uk
CMI (Management Direct Resource Portal) http://www.managers.org.uk/employers/management-
     training-our-services/online-resource-portal
Community Interest Company Regulator http://www.bis.gov.uk/cicregulator/
Companies House www.companieshouse.gov.uk
Co-operatives UK www.uk.coop
Day Nurseries http://www.daynurseries.co.uk/
Her MajestysMajesty's' Revenue & Customs http://www.hmrc.gov.uk/
ICAEW www.businessadviceservice.com
Investors in People UK https://www.investorsinpeople.com
London Councils (2007) *Solving the Quality/Cost Conundrum for London's Childcare Workforce.*
     Available at www.londoncouncils.gov.uk/node/5762, accessed 14 December 2016.
National Council for Voluntary Organisations www.ncvo-vol.org.uk
National Early Years Trainers and Consultants Organisation (NEyTCO) www.neytco.co.uk
National Governors Association (NGA) http://www.nga.org.uk/Home.aspx
NEyTCO http://neytco.co.uk/member-directory/choosing-a-consultant
Pay on Time www.http://payontime.co.uk/
Survey Monkey https://www.surveymonkey.com/
TaxFreeChildcarehttps://www.gov.uk/government/news/tax-free-childcare-top-things-childcare
     -providers-should-know
The Charity Commission www.charity-commission.gov.uk
The Law Society (Lawyers for your Business) www.lawsociety.org.uk/lfyb
The Organisation for Responsible Businesses http://www.orbuk.org.uk/
The Plunkett Foundation www.plunkett.co.uk
UK Government www.gov.uk

NCVO provides the following list of essential staff-related policies (examples of these can be accessed for free from various websites as indicated in the bibliography):

https://www.cipd.co.uk/knowledge/fundamentals/emp-law/harassment/factsheet?IsSrchRes=1
https://knowhownonprofit.org/people/employment-lawand-hr/policies-and-templates/
     healthsafety
https://knowhownonprofit.org/people/employment-law-and-hr/policies-andtemplates/whistle
https://knowhownonprofit.org/people/employment-law-and-hr/policies-and-templates/
     dataprotection
https://www.surreycc.gov.uk/__data/assets/pdf_file/0014/50225/Fire-safety-procedure.Pdf
https://www.surreycc.gov.uk/__data/assets/pdf_file/0012/50223/Emergency-closure-policy.
     pdf
https://www.surreycc.gov.uk/__data/assets/pdf_file/0014/50216/Behaviourmanagement-
policy.pdf
https://www.surreycc.gov.uk/__data/assets/pdf_file/0010/50221/Disposal-of-nappies,-
     aprons-and-glovesprocedure.pdf
https://www.surreycc.gov.uk/__data/assets/pdf_file/0016/50236/Inclusionpolicy-including-
     SEND-and-equality-of-opportunities.pdf

https://www.surreycc.gov.uk/__data/assets/pdf_file/0018/50238/Intimate-care-andtoileting-policy.pdf

https://www.surreycc.gov.uk/__data/assets/pdf_file/0011/50240/Key-person-policy.pdf

https://www.surreycc.gov.uk/__data/assets/pdf_file/0014/50243/Lost-or-missingchild-policy.pdf

https://www.surreycc.gov.uk/__data/assets/pdf_file/0015/50244/Medication-policy.pdf

https://www.surreycc.gov.uk/__data/assets/pdf_file/0016/50245/Nappy-changing-policy.pdf

https://www.surreycc.gov.uk/__data/assets/pdf_file/0013/50251/Operationalprocedure-for-outings.pdf

https://www.surreycc.gov.uk/__data/assets/pdf_file/0015/50253/Risk-assessment-and-risk-benefit-analysis.pdf

https://www.surreycc.gov.uk/__data/assets/pdf_file/0017/50255/Settling-in-policy.pdf

https://www.surreycc.gov.uk/__data/assets/pdf_file/0008/55997/Safeguarding-children-andchild-protection-policy.pdf. [AQ]

https://www.surreycc.gov.uk/__data/assets/pdf_file/0010/50212/Admissions-policy.pdf

https://www.surreycc.gov.uk/__data/assets/pdf_file/0017/50246/Non-attendance-policy.pdf

https://www.surreycc.gov.uk/__data/assets/pdf_file/0018/50247/Non-collectionof-child-policy.pdf

Useful Twitter accounts to follow

Early years organisations

@PACEYchildcare

@NDNAtalk

@Pre_schoolLA

@NEyTCO

@daynurseriesuk

@EYBusiness

@UKchildcareNet

@UKdaynursery

@OfstedBigC

Government departments and agencies

@Ofstednews

@educationgovuk

@hmrcbusiness

@DWP

@ukhomeoffice

@TPRgovuk

@acasorguk

@H_S_E

@CommonsBEIS

Business support and guidance organisations

@acasorguk

@ICAEW_BAS

@CIPD

@ORBOrgUK

@BITC

@cmi_managers

@NGAmedia

@NCVO

@BWBCharitySocEn

@payontime

@e-nation

@SocialEnt_UK

@FSB_Voice

@VirginStartUp

@InBiz4good

@GdnSmallBiz

@smallukbusiness

@ChildcareCCoUk

Your local Enterprise Agency and Chamber of Commerce

Many more can be found by checking out the Lists stored as part of my Twitter profile @jacquiburkefp.

INDEX